THE ORAL LAW

THE ORAL LAW

A STUDY OF
THE RABBINIC CONTRIBUTION TO
TORAH SHE-BE-AL-PEH

by

H. CHAIM SCHIMMEL

Revised Edition

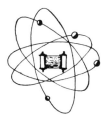

FELDHEIM PUBLISHERS
Jerusalem / New York

To the Memory of My Parents ז"ל

Philipp Feldheim Inc.
200 Airport Executive Park
Spring Valley, NY 10977

Feldheim Publishers Ltd.
POB 6525 / Jerusalem, Israel

Printed in Israel

RABBI MOSES FEINSTEIN
455 F. D. R. DRIVE
New York, N. Y. 10002

—

ORegon 7-1222

משה פיינשטיין
ר"מ תפארת ירושלים
בנוא יארק

בע"ה

הנה בא לפני מהר"ר חיים שיממעל שליט"א מלאנדרן והראה לי ספרו "התורה שבעל פה" ובקש הסכמתי עליו. ובאשר שנכתב בשפת אנגלית, מסרתיו לנכדי, הרה"ג מוהר"ר מרדכי טנדלר שליט"א שקראו לגמרי ושבחו מאד לפני, כספר שמבאר באופן מבואר וקל להבין, בראיות ומקורות, כמה יסודות עיקריות בענין התורה שבעל פה.

ועל כן הריני שולח בזה ברכתי להמחבר שליט"א, שיצליחהו השי"ת בהפרצת ספרו זה, ושיהיה לתועלת להרבות בכלל ישראל ידיעות היסודות אודות תורתינו הקדושה, ושיגרום הרבצת תורה שבזכותה נזכה כולנו בקרוב להרמת קרן התורה ע"י משיח צדקינו.

הכו"ח לכבוד התורה ביום כ"א שבט תשמ"ג בנוא יארק.

משה פיינשטיין

CONTENTS

FOREWORD

When our Sages asserted that "the Holy One, Blessed be He, did not make His covenant with Israel except by virtue of the Oral Law" (*Giṭṭin* 60B), they not only propounded a cardinal Jewish belief, they also expressed a truth as evident today as it was in Talmudic times. The true character of Judaism cannot be appreciated except by an intimate acquaintance with the Oral Law. The Written Law, that is the Five Books of Moses, and even the rest of the Hebrew Bible, we share with other faiths. What makes us and our faith distinct and unique is the oral tradition as the authentic key to an understanding of the written text we call the Torah.

The relations between the Oral and Written Laws may be compared to that between the hard soil of mother earth and the lush vegetation growing from it. The one is rigid and static, in itself lifeless and yet unchanging; the other flexible and dynamic, ever fresh and rejuvenated. The Oral Law exemplifies the covenant with Israel for the very reason that it is in a state of constant renewal. Unlike the Written Law which is fixed like the printed letter, the Oral Law is presented to us in the form of minutes of ongoing discussions between opposing schools of thought, it is energised by the tensions of debate and controversy, and it is steeled in the constant battle of adjusting the time to the Law's organic principles.

Little wonder, therefore, that the most implacable critics of

Judaism and the Jewish way of life come from the ranks of those who have little or no familiarity with the Oral Law. Raised at best on the educational diet of a few chapters of *Chumash*, they can appreciate the true image of Judaism no more than one can recognise a personality by looking at a skeleton.

This contribution of the flesh and blood to the bare bones of Judaism makes the present study by Mr. Harry Schimmel on the Oral Law so valuable.

Well-documented by sources ranging over the entire spectrum of Jewish religious literature, this volume should give the readers some insight into the vitals of Judaism, into what has made it not only the longest living faith but also the subject matter of the most intense study and research over millennia — something entirely without parallel in the world's literature.

May these chapters enhance the appreciation of our heritage and thus strengthen the covenant between God and Israel.

DR. IMMANUEL JAKOBOVITS
Chief Rabbi

PREFACE

Were all the laws of the Oral Torah of Sinaitic origin? If so, how did disputes arise? Why and how are certain laws deduced by the Sages from the Scripture? And what was the practice before such laws had been so deduced? To what extent did the Sages enjoy legislative powers? Why are Rabbinic laws binding? When was the text of the *Mishnah* first settled? And previous to that, how has the law been stated?

This book written by an amateur for amateurs is an attempt to answer some of these problems. I have found that many Yeshivah students, or former Yeshivah students like myself, are puzzled by these problems and they baffle even some Talmudic scholars. I have not made a critical study of the whole subject, but I have attempted to find an answer to these questions in the classical Jewish Literature and in the writings of recognised Rabbinical Authorities.

I had originally undertaken this study for my own benefit. However, the problems I have considered are of importance to anyone who wants to know what Judaism has to teach. In fact, most important conflicts in Judaism, from the Saducees and Pharisees down to the dispute between Orthodox and Reform, are linked with many of these questions. I was encouraged therefore by the "Orthodox Jewish Scientists" to present the fruits of my research to the general public and I have endeavoured to do this in the present book in a form which I hope can readily be absorbed by those who have some acquaintance with Talmudic literature and argument.

The Sinaitic origin of the Oral Law — the principle of *Torah Min Hashomaim* — has been assumed and is the starting point of these investigations. This principle is defined and explained in the chapters of this book, but I have not attempted to probe or prove its correctness.

As far as I am aware, there are a great number of works treating of this subject by writers who have departed from this principle; but a modern book which explains the relationship between the Sinaitic origin of the law and its Rabbinic development, without departing from this principle, is difficult to come by.

The general arrangement of this book is as follows :

In Chapter I, which may be regarded as introductory, we argue that the Oral Law must have originated at the same time as the Written Law and that this can be proven from the Scripture and from various *Mishnayot* (Section I). It is then shown that the Oral Law was further developed by the Sages (Section II) and finally an important distinction is drawn between Sinaitic Law, or more particularly the Oral Law, which originated at the same time as the Written Law, and the law developed later by the Sages (Section III).

Chapter II deals with the laws made by the Sages as interpreters of Sinaitic Law, by the use of "logic" (Section I) and *"drash"* (Section II) and Chapter III with laws newly created by the Sages. In connection with law newly created by the Sages, we discuss when (Section I) and why (Section II) such laws were made, and in the final sections of Chapters II and III we discuss the binding force of the laws considered.

The next two chapters consider the restrictions on the power of the Sages to legislate (Chapter IV) and the question is discussed whether the Sages circumvented these restrictions by the use of legal fictions (Chapter V). The final chapter discusses the work of the Sages in formulating the Oral Law in the Mishnah.

PREFACE

I must in conclusion acknowledge the help I have received in preparing this book.

I am thankful to the Chief Rabbi, Dr. I. Jakobovits, for writing the Foreword to this book.

I am grateful to my friends, Professor Cyril Domb for his constant help and encouragement in the preparation of this book and Mrs. Doreen Rossdale for correcting the final draft. Also to Mr. Alan Smith who took charge of the transliteration and to my Secretary, Miss Frances Jay, who patiently typed and re-typed the various drafts.

My thanks are also due to Mr. Yaakov Feldheim of Feldheim Publishers Limited who has painstakingly made every endeavour to meet my various requirements and to produce this book in an attractive format.

I should also mention Rabbis M. Knoblewitz and B. Hammer, my brother-in-law, Dr. Arnold Schonfeld, and my friends, Mr. H. Abramsky of the Hebrew Department of University College, Mr. C. Abelson, Dr. H. Birnbaum, Mr. L. Carmell, Mr. A. Cohen and Mr. H. Schreiber who read my manuscript and made many useful suggestions.

Finally, should my readers derive any benefit from this book, I presume to refer to my wife, Anna, in the words of Rabbi Akiba "Sheli V'shelachem Shela Hi".

H. S.

PREFACE TO THE FOURTH PRINTING

It gives me great pleasure to think that the work I began more than two decades ago and completed some fifteen years ago, is still in demand and requires a fourth reprinting.

The topic, of course, is 2,000 years old and more, yet each generation has its style and approach. Were it not for the fact that, at Mr. Yaakov Feldheim's suggestion, I am about to publish on related topics, I would have proposed a new edition more in the idiom of the times.

Much has changed in the last twenty years. Thus, for example, were I writing today, I would refer to the *Rambam* and *Ramban* in place of Maimonides and Nachmanides.

There has sprung up a new tradition of writing in English on subjects of *Kedushah* and I trust that I am not quite old enough nor foolish enough to be under the illusion that things were correct only as they were when we were younger. On the contrary, the new generation of Orthodox youth is much to be admired, as are the *Baalei Teshuvah,* of whom we knew little in earlier times.

The publication of Judaica makes an important contribution to the *Teshuvah* movement; to be even a small part of this gives me enormous satisfaction.

As to the substance of the book, I was delighted with the many favorable responses I have had in the press, some well beyond what is deserved. I also had one less favorable review (suppressed, I am pleased to note, by my Publisher). It appeared in the Orthodox Student Journal, *Deot,* and was authored by Prof. Zeev Falk.

After saying it is a "*sefer ofi dugmati shel talmid hacham...*" he complains that no reference is made to such scholars as Frankel Weiss and Tchernowitz.

I did study what these scholars had said, *Da Mah Lehashiv*; however, I have carefully refrained from referring to them for reasons which will be obvious to some. Indeed, much of what I have written was intended to meet their often fanciful misrepresentation of the history of *Torah Sheb'al Peh*.

This reprint carries the Haskamah of Rav Moshe Feinstein. It is now only some months since sadly I must add, *ZTL*.

The only other significant change in the book is, to my sorrow, the dedication to my parents. This reprint is now dedicated to their memory.

יהי זכרונם ברוך.

TRANSLITERATION OF HEBREW ALPHABET

The following system has been used without being too rigid:

b	ב	kh	כ
v	ו	f	פ
ḥ	ח	ẓ	צ
ṭ	ט	k	ק
	t	ת	

Where a traditional Biblical transliteration has become accepted, e.g. Samuel, Esther, Joshua these familiar forms have been retained. Certain other familiar forms such as *Yom Tov, Yeshivah, Halachah,* have also been retained. An apostrophe has occasionally been used to indicate an "Aleph" or "Ayin" but not necessarily.

The abbreviation *Jerus.* refers to the *Jerusalem Talmud (Yerushalmi).*

(The Author is indebted to Mr. Alan Smith for the Transliteration.)

Footnotes which are marked a star thus: **Baba Batra*, are quoted in full under Hebrew Sources at the end of each chapter.

CHAPTER I

THE ORIGIN OF THE ORAL LAW

CHAPTER I

THE ORIGIN OF THE ORAL LAW

INTRODUCTION

The Jewish people are frequently called "The People of the Book", yet if one were to search out a people who follow literally the Bible's behest, one might be led to the Samaritans, who still practise their religion on the outskirts of Shechem, or the Karaites who are now settled to the south of modern Tel-Aviv, but never to the Jewish people. They do not now follow the literal word of the Bible, nor have they ever done so. They have been fashioned and ruled by the verbal interpretation of the written word, more particularly by the "Torah", which embraces both the written and the oral law.

Rabbi D. Z. Hoffman writes as follows :

"The Bible word read from the written book and the teachings heard from the mouth of the Sages are for the Israelite the two sources from which he draws the Torah received by Moses from God on Sinai. The Torah is one, although the source from which it issues is twofold, the teaching which comes to us from the *Mishnah* of the Sages is of the identical date and identical origin as that which is derived by interpretation of the scriptural word, all is given by one God and communicated by one and the same prophet. Hence, when we speak of written law,

Torah She-bikhtab, and oral law, *Torah Sheb'al Peh,* we
have in mind one and the same law of God derived in
part from the divine word committed to writing and in
part from the authoritative statements of the teachers
of tradition." [1]

In this short paragraph, Hoffman sets out one of the fundamental propositions of traditional Judaism which we are about to
examine, namely that the substance of the Oral Law is of Sinaitic
origin. The remainder of this chapter will discuss how in addition
to this substance of the Oral Law which is of Sinaitic origin, there
is the Oral Law which the Sages had not received from Sinai and
which they produced by interpreting the tradition and by creating
new legislation. First, however, we must emphasise the Sinaitic
origin of the Oral Law, because it is important not to lose sight
of the fact that the basic principles of the Oral Law are of Sinaitic
origin and that the law which was *made* rather than revealed takes
only a secondary place. Indeed, it will be shown how the power of
the Sages to make and interpret law stems from the revealed law
and is circumscribed by it. The revealed law reigns supreme notwithstanding the fact that the other law is also part of the divine
law and was made by men inspired by *Ruah Hakodesh,*[2] "so that
they shall not err in their judgment." [3]

1   Hoffman, *Die Erste Mischna* (Berlin, 1882) p.3.
2   *Baba Batra* 12A, *Nachmanides *ad loc.;* Leviticus XXIX, 4; *Nachmanides Deut. XVII; *Divrey Hayyim, Yoreh Deah* II, Responsum 105
"Everyone agrees that *Ruah Hakodesh* did not leave the sages." R.
Jonathan Eibeshutz *Urim Vetumim* quoted by *Hatalmud Umadae
Hatevel,* (Lvow, 1928) p. 111.
3   Leviticus R. XXIX, 4; Chief Rabbi Jakobovits writes "Judaism never
claimed infallibility for its spiritual leaders." *Journal of a Rabbi* (N.Y.
1966) p. 229. See *Tashbaz* II, 9.

*   The full text of all "starred" footnotes is printed in the Hebrew Section
at the end of each chapter.

SECTION I

ORAL LAW OF SINAITIC ORIGIN

It is fortunate that whatever proof there is for the divine origin of the Torah and the Sinaitic origin of the Oral Law it is never quite sufficient to be altogether conclusive. Otherwise, the Jews would have lost a faith and an inner conviction and would have gained a mere science as a substitute.

The Written Law cannot be understood without an Oral Law

Nevertheless, it is possible to show that the written law could never have stood alone and that at the same time as the written law was given at Sinai, it must have been accompanied by an oral tradition.

Hillel attempted to show this, when he was faced by an intending proselyte, who was quite willing to accept the written law, but would not accept the oral tradition. The Talmud [4] in an *Aggadic* passage relates how Hillel showed him that such an attitude was completely untenable, because without an oral tradition it is not possible even to identify the letters of the *Alef-Bet*.

There are two further arguments of which Hillel might have made use:

(I) *That it is difficult, if not impossible, to make sense of the written law without an oral tradition.*

(II) *That there are principles of Oral Law which date from the same time as the written law.*

---

4   *Shabbat* 31A.

I

There are countless terms in the scripture which are undefined, for example the term "work" in sabbatical law, or the term "slaughtering" in *kashrut* law. These are all terms which the Torah uses, but does not define. It does not define what "work"[5] is forbidden or how animals are to be "slaughtered." [6]

There are basic legal concepts and institutions, the existence of which is assumed by the Torah, but which are not further explained. [7] For example, without previously specifying the formalities of marriage and divorce, the Torah states that a first husband cannot re-marry the wife he has divorced, if in the meantime she has been married to another man. [8]

Read without any oral tradition, there are passages in the Bible which appear contradictory. The number of days during which unleavened bread [9] must be eaten on Passover is given as seven in Exodus, [10] but as six in Deuteronomy. [11] The Oral Law [12] explains the discrepancy by stating that the six-day period is one during which the eating of unleavened bread is voluntary, as it is equally permissible to eat potatoes or any other food not containing leavened substance. The seven-day period includes the one day (i.e. the first) on which there is a positive duty to eat *Mazzah*. What meaning have such contradictory passages, without some oral tradition?

Also the fact that the Torah frequently deals with the excep-

5   *Exodus XXXI, 14.
6   *Deut. XII, 21.
7   See Judah Halevi, *Kuzari* III, 35.
8   *Deut. XXIV, 1-4.
9   *Hamez*.
10   Exod. XII, 5.
11   Deut. XVI, 8.
12   *Pesahim* 120A.

tional case, rather than with the principles, indicates the reliance on another statement of law — namely the Oral Law. S.R. Hirsch, the nineteenth century founder of modern German Orthodoxy, in his commentary to the Pentateuch, points out that in the Scripture the civil and criminal law commences with the words "These are the laws which thou shalt put before them" [13] and the Torah immediately proceeds to the laws of slavery. The Torah does not even consider it necessary to begin by stating the laws and principles concerning personal liberty and freedom, because for these principles complete reliance is placed on the Oral Law.

II

The *Mishnah* too yields some evidence of the existence of an Oral Law at the very dawn of Jewish history. There are laws contained in *Mishnayot* which have relevance only to a state of affairs which prevailed before the Jews first settled down in the Land of Israel. [14] We shall mention two examples:

One *Mishnah* [15] deals with leprosy signs which had already appeared upon one of the people *before the Torah was given at Sinai*. It rules that such signs did not render such a person unclean, even after the Torah was given.

Another *Mishnah* [16] deals with the cities which were set aside as a refuge for a man who killed by accident. There were three such cities east of the Jordan, and three in the Land of Israel. The Mishnah rules that *when the Jews first conquered the land* east

---

13 Exodus XXI, 1.
14 The argument developed here and the examples follow Hoffman. *Die Erste Mischna.*
15 *Negaim* VII, 1.
16 *Makkot* II, 4.

of the Jordan, though they appointed cities of refuge there, these
were not operative until all six cities had been designated.

There must already have been an Oral Law in existence at
the time of Sinai and when the Jews reached the Jordan : to argue
otherwise would mean that these laws were formulated at a time
when they no longer applied in practice.

Furthermore, mention should be made of two *Mishnayot* which
deal with problems which arose when the Israelites first reached
the Land of Israel.

The problem of *orlah* (which prohibits the free use of the trees
until the fifth year), and its effect on these first settlers in Israel is
considered by the *Mishnah*. Did the laws of *orlah* apply to trees
which had not been planted by Jews, but were found there when the
Land was conquered? The *Mishnah* [17] rules that *orlah* did not apply,
except in the words of the Scripture "when you come to the land
and plant."

The problem of the daughters of Zelophehad when they first
came to settle in Israel is considered in another *Mishnah*. The fact
that Zelophehad had no male descendents had already given rise
to some problems in the lifetime of Moses [18], when it was ruled
that his property should pass to his daughters. The *Mishnah* [19]
states that the daughters of Zelophehad were entitled to the por-
tion of their father and of their grandfather in the Land of Israel.
The Land was to be divided according to the entitlement of those
who left Egypt (among whom both their father and grandfather
were to be counted) and if they were no longer alive, their descendents took their respective shares.

All these *Mishnayot* indicate that the Oral Law existed from the
very outset of Jewish history. These *Halachot* are almost as old
as the Jewish people themselves. No one with an unprejudiced mind

17   *Orlah* I, 2.
18   Num. XXVII, 1.
19   *Baba Batra* VIII, 3.

would suggest that these *Halachot* were produced after the events to which they relate. It is absurd to suggest that some Sages, centuries after the laws given at Sinai, enacted a law which applied to persons who had leprosy signs before the Torah was given. Who could possibly be affected by such an enactment? So we find Oral Law in existence at the time of Sinai and at the time when the Israelites reached the promised land.

An Oral Law must always have Existed. But what did it Comprise?

These *Mishnayot* show not only that the Oral Law existed at an early date, but also *what the* Oral Law comprised. The evidence of the Scipture itself, where certain apparent deficiencies indicate that there must have been an Oral Law to complement the text, does not show *what* this Oral Law comprised. Those who subscribe to the traditional view claim that this Oral Law was the *Torah Sheb'al Peh* taught by the Sages. Others — like the Saducees — were not prepared to accept that the very *Torah Sheb'al Peh* which the Sages taught was the tradition which had always accompanied the Written Law and which had in fact been handed to Moses by God Himself. They too had to admit that there had always been an Oral Law to explain and expound and supplement the Written Law, but they would argue that the original Oral Law was not one and the same with that taught by the Sages. For traditional Judaism, however, it has always been one of the fundamental tenets that "the teaching which came to us from the *Mishnah* of the Sages is of identical date and origin with that which is derived by interpretation of the Scriptural word, all is given by one God and communicated by one and the same prophet." [20]

20 See Note 1 *ante*.

Talmudic Dicta concerning the Origin of the Oral Law

The *Talmud* and *Midrash* contain a number of statements which affirm that the entire Oral Law, including the *Mishnah* and *Gemara*, originated at Sinai, [21] where it was given by God to Moses. [22] Moses knew all that a conscientious student of the Torah would ever produce in future [23] and when God gave him the Torah, He explained it to him in all its detail. [24]

How do the traditional commentators understand these statements? Maimonides, [25] the great eleventh-century philosopher and codifier, claims that, for example, when God gave the laws of *Sukkah* to Moses, He did not only say "Ye shall dwell in booths seven days." He added that all men (but no women) are obliged to eat, drink and sleep in the *Sukkah;* that the obligation does not apply to those on journeys, or to the sick; that the minimum measurements of the *Sukkah* are 7 by 7 by 10 *tefahim* (handbreadths) and that certain materials are permissible for constructing the roof, and others are not; and that He gave all the other detailed instructions comprised in the Oral Law.

---

21 *Berakhot* 5A.
22 See *Tradition* Vol. 9, Nos. 1 and 2 where Professor Wyshograd discusses the Orthodox view regarding "revelation" and the form in which God "spoke". We would suggest that when the Torah states that God "spoke", it means that the nearest equivalent in human terms to what took place is "speech", because the Torah makes use of human terms to describe superhuman events.
23 *Kohelet* R. I. 9; *Jerus. Peah* II, 4; *Megillah* 19B.
24 *Sifra Behar.* See, however, *Exodus* R. 41, where R. Avia asks rhetorically "and did then Moses learn the entire Torah?" and he replies "No, God taught him only the principles." Also, *Sefer Ha-Ikarim* III, 23, states "It is not possible to claim that God gave the Torah in such a way that it should provide for all times and all events. Moses was given the principles only by means of which the sages of future generations deduced the laws applicable to any situation."
25 *Introduction to Seder Zeraim.*

If that is the case, the question may well be asked "Are not they right who claim that the sages did not make any contribution of their own to the Oral Law?" We shall attempt to answer this question.

SECTION II

ORAL LAW OF RABBINIC ORIGIN

Did the Sages make no contribution to the Oral Law? And was everything they said a mere echo of the tradition they had received at Sinai ?

A View that the Sages never said anything Original — Refuted

In his book *Theology of Ancient Judaism,* [1] Professor Heschel claims that according to some commentators, the Sages contributed nothing original to the Oral Law: "The Sages of the Talmud never said anything which they had not received by tradition from Sinai." However, on looking at the authorities quoted in his footnotes, one feels that Heschel has misled himself.

The View of Rabenu Hananel

R. Hananel, a tenth-century Biblical and Talmudic commentator, is Heschel's first authority. In order to understand what he says, it is necessary to consider the following Talmudic problem. The Talmud [2] is faced by two apparently contradictory statements:

1   Soncino Press, 1962, Vol.II, p. 245.
2   *Sukkah* **45B.**

1. A statement by the second century *Tanna*, R. Simon b. Yohai, that those who receive God's presence are only a few.

2. A statement by the fourth century *Amora*,[3] Raba, that there are 18,000 who receive God's presence?"

The Talmud accordingly questions the contradiction, "How can R. Simon say that there are only a few when Raba said there are 18,000 who receive God's presence"?

So much for our Talmudic problem. R. Hananel,[4] with whose comments on this we are here concerned, has a different problem. He asks "How can the Talmud challenge a statement of R. Simon b. Yohai because it contradicts something said centuries later by another of the Sages? Was he to take into consideration in the second century what Raba would be saying in the fourth century?" To this R. Hananel gives the following answer: The words of Raba "merely record a tradition already known to the rabbis ... because these statements and others like them cannot be made except when received through the prophets."

Heschel would like to read into R. Hananel's words the idea that none of the Sages ever made a statement which they had not received by tradition. However, this cannot be correct, because R. Hananel's statement is qualified by the words *"these statements and others like them,"* words which clearly indicate that he is of the view that the Sages *did* make statements of their own accord. "These statements and others like them" are exceptional, because they deal with a celestial mystery — the question of receiving God's presence. In such matters, the Sages would not speak of their own accord or say anything which they had not "received through the prophets."

3   *"Tanna"* is a teacher quoted in the *Mishnah* or *Baraita*, in contra-distinction to *"Amora"*, who is a teacher whose discussion on the *Mishnah* is reported in the *Gemara*.

4   **Sukkah* 45B.

The View of Ra'abad

The other authority referred to in Heschel's footnotes is Ra'abad, the twelfth century Spanish Talmudist, who writes [5] "the Sages of the Talmud and certainly those of the Mishnah never said even a small thing of their own accord, except *Takkanot*, which they instituted anonymously, in order to create a fence round the Torah."

Here indeed there would have been support for Heschel's contention, were it not for the fact that Ra'abad immediately goes on to say [6] "the Sages never had any dispute regarding the principle of any *Mizvah*, their disputes concerned the details only"; and now come the operative words "they had heard the principles from their teachers, and had not enquired about the details." Clearly then, according to Ra'abad, a substantial part of the Talmud which deals with the detailed application of the *Mizvot* comprises statements of the Sages not based on information their teachers had received from Sinai, but based on their own understanding of what the law should be, having regard to the principles they had received from their teachers.

Our purpose in quoting these authorities at length is not only to disprove Heschel's argument, but also to support, with the very authorities which Heschel misunderstood, our own contention; namely, that the Sages contributed views, statements and *Halachot* of their own.

Indeed the very idea that the entire Oral Law was communicated to Moses is expressed in the words "Moses knew all that a conscientious student would produce (*Mehadesh*) in future," [6a] which indicate further developments of the Law after the time of Moses.

5   *Sefer Hakabbala* (Messora Press, Jerusalem, 1956) p. 1.
6   This is not quoted by Heschel.
6A According to one reading of Leviticus R. XXII (1) quoted by Heschel *op. cit. p.* 236 Note 10. See also *Megillah* 19B.

The proposition that the Sages did make original contributions to the Oral Law brings us to another problem : Does this contradict the statement that the entire Oral Law was communicated by God to Moses at Sinai?

Moses did not hand down all the Oral Law he had received

There are at least two possible solutions. One is to suggest that although the entire Oral Law was communicated to Moses at Sinai, Moses did not pass it all on to future generations. In fact, the Jerusalem Talmud [7] suggests that Moses was not permitted to pass on the entire Oral Law to others. Accordingly, whereas Moses received the entire Oral Law at Sinai, he did not communicate it all to Joshua, his disciple, because he was not allowed to do so.

Much that was taught was later forgotten

Another solution lies in the natural erosion caused by the passage of time. [8] Possibly, in the fulness of time, much that Moses had passed on was forgotten. The Talmud [9] reports that Joshua was made to forget three hundred laws as a punishment for a proud answer he once gave to Moses. Shortly before his death, Moses invited him to clear up any doubt which he might have regarding Halachah. The latter gave the proud answer "I have no difficulties" and forgot three hundred *Halachot* on that day. Moreover, it would appear that forgetfulness was a penalty exacted from

7   *Jerus. Aboda Zara;* and see also *Megillat Esther, Sefer Hamizvoth, Shoresh Alef* (Note 16) and R. Yomtov Lipman, *Introduction to Tosefot Yom-Tov, Massekhet Berakhot.*
8   See Ḥazon Ish. *Collected Letters* (B'nei B'rak, 1956) Part II, p. 24, "The Sages produced again what had been forgotten."
9   *Temurah* 16A.

later generations too, on account of their lack of humility. Had they only had sufficient humility to listen carefully to their elders and diligently absorb their teachings, there would never have been any doubts or controversies regarding the law. As it was, the Talmud reports that the pupils of Hillel and Shammai did not serve their masters as much as was necessary and consequently the number of doubts and controversies increased. [10]

The Talmud [11] also reports that their master, Hillel, had made a similar complaint against the leaders of his own generation. Had they only listened sufficiently to Shmaya and Abtalyon, the two great teachers, they would not have been in doubt regarding the *Halachah*. It may be assumed that all generations were beset by forgetfulness [12] and consequently, the Oral Law, communicated entire to Moses at Sinai, by the period of the Sages was incomplete. There were many gaps which remained to be filled, and they were filled by the original contributions of the Sages.

The two categories of law, those which originated at Sinai and those made by the Sages, together formed the *Torah Sheb'al Peh* which is part of the divine law of God. There is a clear distinction in the nature of the two types of law.

Maimonides [13] explains that the Oral Law received by the Sages in a direct chain of tradition from Sinai remained for all time clear and certain, free from doubt and controversy, whereas the law which did not come by way of tradition was beset by a great number of disputes; we will discuss this distinction in greater detail.

10 *Sanhedrin* 88B, *Sotah* 47B
11 *Pesahim* 66A.
12 See *Sukkah* 20A and *Yoma* 81A, *Shabbat* 104A, *Sukkah* 44A.
13 *Introduction to Seder Zeraim.*

SECTION III

THE TWO TYPES OF LAW DISTINGUISHED AND THE ORIGIN OF DISPUTES

While Sanhedrin functioned there were no Disputes

No disputes between the Sages were recorded in early times. If any disputes arose which concerned a matter of law it was soon settled. The Talmud states [1] that all controversies were referred to the Sanhedrin where they were put to the vote. For example, if a question of ritual cleanness was involved then "if the majority voted unclean, they declared it so, if clean, they ruled even so." In the result, as long as the Sanhedrin existed, no disputes were recorded. The Oral Law spoke with a single voice on every issue. No records had to be kept of the different views, because once the Sanhedrin had decided the *Halachah,* there was only one view that mattered, namely, that which accorded with the decision of the majority. [2] When, however, political conditions no longer allowed

---

1   *Sanhedrin* 88B.
2   With regard to these early laws, there is only one recorded dispute which remained unsettled. It arose in the following circumstances *(Ḥagigah* II, 2). Normally, the Torah required a person to lay hands on his Temple sacrifice (Levit. I, 4). On Sabbath and *Yom Tov,* however, the Sages had forbidden the handling of animals. The question then arose whether or not the Rabbinic prohibition against handling animals on *Yom Tov* applied even in this case, when the handling of the animals was required in order to comply with the ritual which the Torah had prescribed for sacrifices. This question divided the Sanhedrin for five generations, the *Nasi* taking the one view and the President of the Court the other. No one can say with certainty why this controversy was not resolved, in the same way as the other disputes.

a Sanhedrin to function — in the time of Hillel and Shammai — separate schools arose, each having its own view, and there was no forum in which these disputes could be resolved.

Even after Sanhedrin ceased, Sinaitic Law remained free from Disputes

However, the position was different regarding Sinaitic laws. The Oral Law which had been transmitted in a chain of tradition from Sinai remained for all time free from controversy and doubt. There was no question of settling disputes, because disputes could never arise. If, in the course of a Talmudic argument, one of the Sages expressed a view that a certain law seemed to him to be open to objection he would usually take care to add that if that law was based on tradition he would accept it. [3] But even without adding this rider, it was understood that a law could not be challenged if it had been received in a direct line of transmission from Sinai, and so such laws remained for all time free from doubt and controversy.

The Classification of Maimonides

What has been said so far is of the greatest importance in the classification adopted by Maimonides. [4] For he draws this clear distinction between the two types of law, those which are of Sinaitic origin and which are not subject to controversy, and those not of Sinaitic origin, which are subject to controversy. In this classification, the Sinaitic laws consists of:

3   *Negaim* IX, 3 and XI, 7; *Yebamot* VIII, 3; *Kritot* III, 9.
4   *Introduction to Seder Zeraim.*

(i) Interpretations received at Sinai of the Scripture

(ii) *Halacha Le Moshe Misinai.*

Non-Sinaitic Laws consist of:

(i) Laws derived by the Sages [5]

(ii) *Takkanot* and *Gezerot.*[6]

Problems concerning Halachah Le Moshe Misinai

More will be said about this classification in the next chapter with particular reference to the non-Sinaitic laws. Here we will add only a few remarks concerning *Halachah Le Moshe Misinai.* As Maimonides defines this term, it applies to laws which have no intrinsic connection with the Scripture, but are of Sinaitic origin. This is its strict technical meaning, although the term is sometimes used more loosely to describe laws which are of long standing, even though they are not of Sinaitic origin. [7]

This definition of Maimonides has been much criticised for two reasons. Firstly, according to Maimonides, laws of Sinaitic origin are not subject to controversy, yet there are a number of controversies in the Talmud concerning *Halachah Le Moshe Misinai.*[8] Secondly, according to Maimonides, laws classed as *Halachah Le Moshe Misinai* are distinguished by not having any intrinsic connection with

---

5   The Sages derived laws by means of *drash* and logic. See next chapter.

6   See Chapter III for *Takkanot* and *Gezerot.*

7   *Yadayim* IV, 3, Bartenura, *ad. loc.;* Rosh, *Introduction to Mikva'ot.*

8   See R. Ḥayyim Bachrach in *Ḥavot Yair* Responsum 192 who cites many cases of controversy concerning *Halachah Le Moshe Misinai.* It seems, however, that disputes in *Halachah Le Moshe Misinai* concern only details which do not go to the root of the law. There is no case of *Halachah Le Moshe Misinai;* one *Tanna* declaring an object *Kasher* or an act permitted and another declaring the identical object or act prohibited.

the Scripture, yet the Talmud describes certain laws as *Halachah Le Moshe Misinai* and still connects them *Midrashically* with the Scripture.[9]

---

9   *Shabbat* 103B; *Erubin* 4B. Maimonides, *Commentary Sukkah*, IV, 9, distinguishes between an open *Remez* (allusion) and one that is hidden (or merely an *Asmakhta*). See also *Megillat Esther, Sefer Hamizvot, Shoresh* I.

HEBREW SOURCES

(The numbers correspond to the relevant footnotes)

SECTION I

RUAḤ HAKODESH INSPIRED THE SAGES IN THEIR LAW MAKING

2.   *Baba Batra* 12A

אמר רבי אבדימי דמן חיפה, מיום שחרב בית המקדש ניטלה נבואה מן
הנביאים וניתנה לחכמים.

Nachmanides, *loc. cit.*

הכי קאמר, אעפ"י שנטלה נבואת הנביאים שהוא המראה והחזון, נבואת
החכמים שהיא בדרך החכמה לא נטלה, אלא יודעים האמת ברוח הקדש
שבקרבם.

Nachmanides, Deut. XVII, 11

אפילו יהיה בעיניך כ(אילו החכם) מחליף הימין בשמאל, וכל שכן שיש
לך לחשוב שהם אומרים על ימין שהוא ימין. כי רוח השם על משרתי מקדשו,
ולא יעזוב את חסידיו לעולם נשמרו מן הטעות ומן המכשול.

R. Jonathan Eibeshutz, *Urim Vetumim*

מרן הגאון הרבי ר' יונתן זצ"ל בספרו "אורים ותומים" יאמר, דמה שמוכיחים
לפעמים איזה דין מחודש ואיזה סברא חדשה מדברי חז"ל מדמשני הכי, ולא

משני באופן אחר, שמע מינה דאין הדין כן כמו שנראה מאופן האחר שעלה בדעתנו
ליישב, כל זה הוא מפני שהתהלמוד ברוח הקודש נאמר, ואילו היה אפשר
לתרץ באופן זה בודאי זה היו מרגישים גם המה מזה האופן, ואם חז"ל לא הביאו
אופן זה ותירצו באופן האמור בגמרא, זה האות שהאופן שלנו שעלה בדעתנו
לא נכון הוא ואינה לאמיתה של תורה.

TERMS WHICH ARE NOT DEFINED IN THE TORAH

5.   Exod. XXXI, 14

ושמרתם את השבת כי קדש הוא לכם מחלליה מות יומת כי כל ה ע ש ה
ב ה מ ל א כ ה ונכרתה הנפש ההוא מקרב עמיה.

6.   Deut. XII, 21

כי ירחק ממך המקום אשר יבחר ה' אלוקיך לשום שמו שם ו ז ב ח ת מ ב ק ר ך
ו מ צ א נ ך א ש ר נ ת ן ה ' ל ך כ א ש ר צ ו י ת ך . ואכלת בשעריך בכל
אות נפשך.

7.   Juda Halevy, *Kuzari* III, 35

אמר הכוזרי: כן אומרים הקראים אבל אחר שמצאו התורה שלמה אינם
צריכים אל הקבלה.

אמר החבר: ..התראה כאשר אמר להם: החדש הזה לכם ראש חדשים על
הדמיון לא נסתפק העם אם רצה לומר: חדשי המצרים שהיו ביניהם או
חדשי כשדים שהיו עם אברהם באור כשדים, או רצה חדשי השמש או חדשי
הירח... ומה ענין הזביחה ושמא היא נחירה או הרג....

והייתי רוצה שיבאר לי החלב האסור והוא דבק עם המותר במעים והקיבה.
....והייתי רוצה שיבאר לי העוף הטהור מן הטמא, זולת המפורסמים,
רצוני לומר: בן-יונה או תור, ומאין הוא אומר שאין התרנגולת והאוז והקורא
ואלברכיה מהטמאים. והייתי רוצה שיתן לי גבול, אל יצא איש ממקומו ביום
השבת, אם הוא ביתו או חצירו או רשותו....

8. Deut. XXIV, 1—4

כי יקח איש אשה ובעלה והיה אם לא תמצא־חן בעיניו כי מצא בה
ערות דבר וכתב לה ספר כריתת ונתן בידה ושלחה מביתו. ויצאה
מביתו והלכה והיתה לאיש אחר. ושנאה האיש האחרון וכתב לה ספר כריתת
ונתן בידה ושלחה מביתו או כי ימות האיש האחרון אשר לקחה לו לאשה.
לא יוכל בעלה הראשון אשר שלחה לשוב לקחתה להיות לו לאשה אחרי אשר
הטמאה כי תועבה הוא לפני ה' ולא תחטיא את הארץ אשר ה' א' נתן לך
נחלה.

OLD LAWS IN THE *MISHNAH*

15. *Negaim* VII, 1

אלו בהרות טהורות. שהיו בו קודם למתן תורה. (מי שהיתה בו צרעת
קודם מתן תורה לא היה טמא מחמת אותו נגע לאחר מתן תורה. (ר"ע
מברטנורה).

16. *Makkot* II, 4

להיכן גולין, לערי מקלט. לשלש שבעבר הירדן ולשלש שבארץ כנען.
שנאמר (במדבר ל"ה) את שלש הערים תתנו מעבר לירדן ואת שלש הערים
תתנו בארץ כנען וגו'.
עד שלא נבחרו שלש שבארץ ישראל, לא היו שלש בעבר הירדן קולטות.

17. *Orlah* I, 2

עת שבאו אבותינו לארץ, מצאו נטוע פטור, נטעו אע"פ שלא כבשו חייב.

19. *Baba Batra* VIII, 3

בנות צלפחד נטלו שלשה חלקים בנחלה. חלק אביהן שהיה עם יוצאי
מצרים וחלקו עם אחיו בנכסי חפר ושהיה בכור נוטל שני חלקים.

THE ENTIRE ORAL LAW ORIGINATED AT SINAI

21. *Berakhot* 5A

וא"ר לוי בר חמא אמר ר' שמעון בן לקיש, מאי דכתיב "ואתנה לך את לוחות האבן והתורה והמצוה אשר כתבתי להורותם". "לוחות" אלו עשרת הדברות, "תורה" זה מקרא, "והמצוה" זו משנה, "אשר כתבתי" אלו נביאים וכתובים, "להורותם" זה גמרא, מלמד שכולם נתנו למשה מסיני.

23. *Jerus. Peah* II, 4

מקרא, משנה, תלמוד ואגדה, אפי' מה שתלמיד ותיק עתיד להורות לפני רבו כבר נאמר למשה בסיני.

23. *Megillah* 19B

מלמד שהראהו הקב"ה למשה דקדוקי תורה ודקדוקי סופרים ומה שהסופרים עתידין לחדש.

24. *Sifra Behar*

וידבר ה' אל משה בהר סיני לאמר מה ענין שמיטה אצל הר סיני והלא כל המצות נאמרו מסיני, אלא מה שמטה שנאמרו כללותיה ודקדוקיה מסיני, אף כולם נאמרו כללותיהם ודקדוקיהם מסיני.

25. Maimonides, *Introduction to Seder Zeraim*

והנה לך משל : הקדוש־ברוך הוא אמר למשה : בסכת תשבו שבעת ימים (ויקרא כ"ג מ"ב) אחר כן הודיע שהסכה הזאת חובה על הזכרים לא על הנקבות. ושאין החולים חייבין בה ולא הולכי דרך ושלא יהיה סכוכה אלא בצמח הארץ ולא יסככנה בצמר ולא במשי ולא בכלים — אפילו מאשר תצמיח הארץ כגון הכסתות והכרים והבגדים. והודיע שהאכילה והשתיה והשינה בה כל שבעה — חובה ; ושלא יהיה בחללה פחות משבעה טפחים ארך על שבעה טפחים רוחב ; ושלא יהיה גובה הסכה פחות מעשרה טפחים.

SECTION II

THE SAGES CONTRIBUTED STATEMENTS AND *HALACHOT*
OF THEIR OWN ACCORD

2. *Sukkah* 45B

ואמר חזקיה א״ר ירמיה משום רשב״י ראיתי בני עלייה והן מועטין אם אלף
הן אני ובני מהן. אם מאה הן אני ובני מהן.אם שנים הן אני ובני הן. ומי
זוטרי כולי האי ?

והא אמר רבא תמני סרי אלפי דרא הוה דקמיה קודשא בריך הוא שנאמר
"סביב שמנה עשר אלף" (יחזקאל מ״ח) לא קשיא הא דמסתכלי באספקלריא
המאירה הא דלא מסתכלי באספקלריה המאירה. ודמסתכלי באספקלריא המאירה
מי זוטרי כולי האי ? והא אמר אביי לא פחות עלמא מתלתין ושיתא צדיקי
דמקבלי אפי שכינה בכל יום ?

4. *R. Hananel, ad. loc.*

והלא אביי ורבא דאחרונים הן לגבי רשב״י ואיך מקשינן מדבריהם עליו ?
אלא ללמדך המסורת שהיה בידם בדברי אביי ורבא כך היה בידי הראשונים
בקבלה כהל״מ. ואינם דבריהם, שאלו הדברים וכיוצא בהן אי
אפשר להאמר אלא בקבלה מן הנביאים ואלו הדברים שקיבלו מרבותיהם היו
מגידין.

5. *Ra'abad, Sefer Hakabbalah*

זה ספר הקבלה כתבנוהו להודיע לתלמידים כי כל דברי רבותינו ז״ל
חכמי המשנה והתלמוד כולם מקובלים חכם גדול וצדיק מפי חכם גדול וצדיק.
ראש ישיבה וסיעתו מפי ראש ישיבה וסיעתו מאנשי כנסת הגדולה שקבלו
מהנביאים זכר כולם לברכה. ולעולם חכמי התלמוד וכל שכן חכמי המשנה
אפילו דבר קטן לא אמרו מלבם חוץ מן התקנות שתקנו בהסכמת כולם כדי
לעשות סייג לתורה.

ואם לחשך אדם לומר מפני שנחלקו בכמה מקומות לכך אני מסופק בדבריהם
אף אתה הקהה את שיניו והודיעהו שהוא ממרה על פי בי״ד ושלא נחלקו
רז״ל לעולם מצוה בעיקר אלא בתולדותיה ששמעו עיקרה מרבותיהם ולא
שאלום על תולדותיה מפני שלא שמשו כל צרכן. כיוצא בו לא נחלקו אם
מדליקין נר בשבת או לא ועל מה נחלקו במה מדליקין ובמה אין מדליקין.

MOSES DID NOT COMMUNICATE THE ENTIRE ORAL LAW

7. *Jerus. Aboda Zara* II, 7

א״ר יצחק כתיב ״ואותי צוה ה״״ (דברים ד') אותי ואותי נאמר לי דברים
שנאמר לכם ונאמר לי דברים שנאמר בינו לבין עצמי.

7. Yomtov Lipman, *Introduction to Tosefot Yom-Tov Berakhot*

אבל תועלת חבור המשנה וסיבתה היתה לפי שתורה שבע״פ שמסרה
משה ליהושע ויהושע לזקנים וכו', אע״פ שהיתה ביאור התורה ומצוותיה
ביאור שלם. אין לך זמן ודור שלא יתחדש בהכרח ויפלא למשפט. ואל תשיבני
דבר ממה שאמרו בפ״ב דמגילה (יט :) מאי ועליהם ככל הדברים וכו'. מלמד
שהראהו הקב״ה למשה דקדוקי תורה ודקדוקי סופרים ע״כ. שאני אומר שזה
לא היה מוסר משה לאחרים כלל. ודקדוק לשונם כך הוא שאמרו מלמד שהראהו
ולא אמר שמסר לו או שלמדו.

IN THE FULNESS OF TIME MUCH LAW WAS FORGOTTEN

9. *Temurah* 16A

אמר רב יהודה אמר רב : בשעה שנפטר משה רבנו לגן עדן אמר לו
ליהושע שאל ממני כל ספקות שיש לך אמר לו רבי כלום הנחתיך שעה אחת
והלכתי למקום אחר לא כך כתבת בי ״ומשרתו יהושע בן נון נער לא ימיש
מתוך האהל (שמות ל״ג)״ מיד תשש כחו של יהושע ונשתחכו ממנו שלש
מאות הלכות ונולדו לו שבע מאות ספיקות ....
במתניתין תנא אלף ושבע מאות קלין וחמורין וגזירות שוות ודקדוקי סופרים
נשתכחו בימי אבלו של משה. אמר רבי אבהו אעפ״כ החזירן עתניאל בן קנז
מתוך פלפולו.

12. *Sukkah* 20A

שבתחילה כשנשתכחה תורה מישראל עלה עזרא מבבל ויסדה, חזרה ונשתכחה
עלה הלל הבבלי ויסדה, חזרה ונשתכחה עלו רבי חייא ובניו ויסדוה.

SECTION III

IN EARLY TIMES NO DISPUTES BETWEEN THE SAGES
WERE RECORDED

1. *Sanhedrin* 88B

אמר ר' יוסי מתחילה לא היו מרבין מחלוקת בישראל. אלא בית דין של
שבעים ואחד יושבין בלשכת הגזית ושני בתי דינין של עשרים ושלושה
אחד יושב על פתח הר הבית ואחד יושב על פתח העזרה ושאר בתי דינין של
עשרים ושלשה יושבין בכל עיירות ישראל הוצרך הדבר לשאל שואלין מבית
דין שבעירן אם שמעו אמרו להן ואם לאו באין לזה שסמוך לעירן אם שמעו
אמרו להם ואם לאו באין לזה שעל פתח הר הבית אם שמעו אמרו להם
ואם לאו באין לזה שעל פתח העזרה, ואומר כך דרשתי וכך דרשו חברי כך
למדתי וכך למדו חברי אם שמעו אמרו להם ואם לאו אלו ואלו באין ללשכת
הגזית, ששם יושבין מתמיד של שחר עד תמיד של בין הערבים ובשבתות
ובימים טובים יושבין בחיל. נשאלה שאלה בפניהם אם שמעו אמרו להם ואם
לאו עומדין למנין רבו המטמאים טמאו רבו המטהרין טהרו. משרבו תלמידי
שמאי והלל שלא שמשו כל צרכן רבו מחלוקת בישראל ונעשית תורה כשתי
תורות.

THE ONLY RECORDED DISPUTE WHICH REMAINED UNSETTLED

2. *Ḥagigah* II, 2

יוסי בן יועזר אומר שלא לסמוך. יוסי בן יוחנן אומר לסמוך. יהושע בן
פרחיה אומר שלא לסמוך. ניתאי הארבלי אומר לסמוך. יהודה בן טבאי אומר
שלא לסמוך. שמעון בן־שטח אומר לסמוך. שמעיה אומר לסמוך. אבטליון
אומר שלא לסמוך.
הלל ומנחם לא נחלקו. יצא מנחם נכנס שמאי, שמאי אומר שלא לסמוך.
הלל אומר לסמוך. הראשונים היו נשיאים ושניים להם אבות בית דין.

A LAW BASED ON TRADITION WAS ALWAYS. ACCEPTED

3. *Yebamot* VIII, 3

עמוני ומואבי אסורים. ואיסורן איסור עולם. אבל נקבותיהם מותרת מיד.
מצרי ואדומי אינם אסורים אלא עד שלושה דורות אחד זכרים ואחד נקבות.
רבי שמעון מתיר את הנקבות מיד. אמר רבי שמעון קל וחומר הדברים. ומה
אם במקום שאסר את הזכרים איסור עולם התיר את הנקבות מיד. מקום שלא
אסר את הזכרים אלא עד ג׳ דורות אינו דין שנתיר את הנקבות מיד. אמרו
לו אם הלכה נקבל ואם לדין יש תשובה.

THE CLASSIFICATION OF MAIMONIDES

4. *Introduction to Seder Zeraim*

ה ח ל ק   ה ר א ש ו ן — פרושים מקובלים מפי משה ויש להם רמז בכתוב,
ואפשר להוציאם בדרך סברא — וזה אין בו מחלוקת אבל כשיאמר האחד
"כך קבלתי" — אין לדבר עליו.

ה ח ל ק   ה ש נ י — הדינים שנאמר בהם: "הלכה למשה מסיני" ואין ראיות
עליהם כמו שזכרנו, וזה כמו כן — אין חולק עליו.

ה ח ל ק   ה ש ל י ש י — הדינין שהוציאו על דרכי הסברא ונפלה בם מחלקת,
כמו שזכרנו, ונפסק הדין בהם על-פי הרב. וזה יקרה — כשישתנה העיון. ומפני
כך אומרים: "אם הלכה — נקבל, ואם לדין — יש תשובה". אבל, נפלה המחלוקת
והעיון בדבר שלא נשמע בו הלכה. ותמצא בכל-התלמוד שהם חוקרים על
טעם הסברא שהוא גורם המחלוקת בין החולקים ואומרים: "במאי קא-
מפלגי"? או "מאי טעמא דרבי פלוני"? או "מאי ביניהו"? והם מביאים
אותו על ענין זה ברב מקומות, וזוכרים הטעם הגורם למחלוקת, כגון שיאמרו:
רבי פלוני מחזיק טענה פלונית, ופלוני מחזיק טענה פלונית וכדומה לו.

אבל מי שיחשוב: שהדינים שנחלקים בהם, כמו-כן מקובלים מפי משה
וחושבים שנפלה המחלקת מדרך טעות ההלכות, או השכחה, או מפני שאחד
מהם קיבל קבלת אמת והשני טעה בקבלתו, או שכח או לא שמע מפי רבו
כל מה-שצריך לשמוע; ויביא ראיה על זה ממה-שאמרו: "משרבו תלמידי
שמאי והלל שלא שמשו כל-צרכם, רבתה המחלוקת בישראל ונעשית תורה

כשתי תורות" — דברים כאלה הם, חי נפשי, דברים מגונים ומכוערים מאד. והנם
דברי מי שאין לו ידיעה ואין בידו העיקרים, ופוגם באנשים אשר נתקבלו מהם
המצוות — וכל־זה שוא ובטל. ומה־שהביאו להאמין באמונה הזאת הנפסדת
הוא : מעוט הסתכלותו בדברי החכמים הנמצאים בתלמוד. שהם מצאו : שכל־
הפרוש מקובל מפי משה והוא אמת ; ולא נתנו הפרש בין "העקרים המקובלים"
ובין תולדות העניינים שיוציאו אותם בעיון. אבל, אתה, אל יכנס בלבך ספק
במחלוקת בית־שמאי ובית־הלל באמרם : "מכבדין את הבית ואחר־כך נוטלים
לידים ; או נוטלים לידים ואחר־כך מכבדין את הבית", ותחשוב שאחד משני
הדברים האלו אינו מקובל מפי משה מסיני — אבל הטעם שהוא גורם להיות
חולקים, הוא מה־שנזכר בתלמוד : שאחד מהם אוסר להשתמש בעם־הארץ
והשני מתיר. וכן כל מה־שידמה לאלו המחלוקות שהם ענפים מענפי הענפים.

אבל מה־שאמרו : "משרבו תלמידי שמאי והלל שלא שמשו כל־צרכם רבתה
מחלוקת בישראל" — ענין זה מבואר : שכל שני אנשים בהיותם שוים בשכל
ובעיון ובידיעת "העיקרים" שיוציאו מהם הסברות, לא תפול ביניהם מחלוקת
בסברתם בשום פנים ; ואם נפלה — תהיה מעוטה, כמו שלא נמצא שנחלקו
שמאי והלל אלא בהלכות יחידות ; וזה — מפני שדעות שניהם היו קרובות
זו לזו בכל־מה־שהוציאו בדרך סברא. והעיקרים, כמו כן, הנתונים לזה כמו
העיקרים הנתונים לזה. אבל כאשר רפתה שקידת התלמידים על החכמה ונחלשה
סברתם כנגד סברת הלל ושמאי רבותיהם — נפלה מחלוקת ביניהם בעיון על
דברים רבים שסברת כל־אחד ואחד מהם היתה לפי שכלו ולפי מה־שיש בידו
מן־העיקרים. ואין להאשימם בכל־זאת — שלא נכריח אנחנו לשני חכמים
מתוכחים בעיון להתוכח בשכל יהושע ופנחס. ואין לנו ספק כמו־כן במה־
שנחלקו בו, מאחר שאינם כמו שמאי והלל, או כמי שהוא למעלה מהם —
שהקדוש־ברוך־הוא לא צונו בעבודתו על ענין זה ; אבל צונו לשמוע מחכמי
הדור, כמו שאמר : ואל־השופט אשר יהיה בימים ההם (דברים יז, ט). ועל־
הדרכים האלו נפלה המחלוקת ; לא מפני שטעו בהלכות ושהאחד אומר אמת,
והשני — שקר. ומה־מאד מבואר ענין זה לכל־המסתכל בו, ומה־יקר וגדול
זה העיקר במצוות !

וההלק הרביעי — הם הדינים שתקנו הנביאים והחכמים בכל־דור ודור,
כדי לעשות סיג וגדר לתורה. ועליהם צוה הקדוש־ברוך־הוא לעשותם, והוא
מה־שאמר במאמר כללי : ושמרתם את משמרתי (ויקרא יח, ל), ובאה בו
הקבלה : "עשו משמרת למשמרתי". והחכמים יקראו אותם : "גזרות". ולפעמים
תפול בהם מחלוקת — לפי שחכם אחד ראה לגזור כך, ולא יסכים עליו חכם

אחר. וזה הרבה בתלמוד שאומרים: רבי פלוני גזר כך משום כך וכך, ורבי
פלוני לא גזר. וזה כמו כן סיבת המחלוקות. שהרי בשר עוף בחלב
היא גזירה מדרבנן, כדי להרחיק מן־העבירה, ולא נאסר בתורה אלא בשר
בהמה טהורה; אבל אסרו חכמים בשר עוף — כדי להרחיק מן־האיסור. ויש
מהם מי שלא יגזור גזירה זו: שרבי־יוסי־הגלילי היה מתיר בשר עוף בחלב,
וכל־אנשי עירו היו אוכלים אותו, כמו שנתפרסם בתלמוד. וכשתפול הסכמה
על־אחת מן־הגזירות — אין חולקין עליה בשום פנים; וכשיהיה איסורה פשוט
בכל ישראל — אין לחלוק על־הגזירה ההיא. ואפילו הנביאים בעצמם לא היו
רשאים לבטל אותה. וכן אמרו בתלמוד: "שאליהו, זכור לטוב, לא היה יכול
לבטל אחד משמונה־עשר דבר שגזרו בית־שמאי ובית־הלל. והביאו טעם על־
זה: "לפי שאיסורם פשט בכל־ישראל".

והחלק החמישי — הם הדינים העשויים על דרך החקירה וההסכמה
בדברים הנוהגים בין בני אדם, שאין בם תוספת במצוה ולא גרעון; או בדברים
שהם תועלת לבני אדם בדברי תורה, וקראו אותם: "תקנות ומנהגים", ואסור לעבור
עליהם. וכבר אמר שלמה, עליו־השלום, על־העובר עליהם: ופורץ גדר ישכנו
נחש (קהלת י ח). ואלו התקנות רבות מאד ונזכרות בתלמוד ובמשנה: מהן —
בענין איסור והתר; ומהן — בענין הממונות; ומהן — תקנות שתיקנו נביאים,
כמו תקנות משה ויהושע ועזרא, כמו שאמרו: "משה תיקן להם לישראל
שיהיו שואלים ודורשים בהלכות פסח בפסח". ואמרו: "משה תיקן 'הזן' בשעה
שירד המן לישראל". אבל תקנות יהושע ועזרא הן רבות. ומהן — תקנות
מיוחסות ליחידים מן־החכמים, כמו שאמרו: "התקין הלל פרוזבול"; "התקין
רבן־גמליאל־הזקן"; "התקין רבן־יוחנן־בן־זכאי". והרבה בתלמוד: "התקין רבי
פלוני", "התקין רבי פלוני". ויש מהן תקנות מיוחסות להמון החכמים כמו
שאמרו: "באושא התקינו", או כמו שאמרו: "תקנו חכמים" או "תקנות
חכמים" וכדומה לזה הרבה.

CHAPTER II

LAWS DERIVED BY RABBINIC INTERPRETATION

CHAPTER II

LAWS DERIVED BY RABBINIC INTERPRETATION

INTRODUCTION

Although, as has been seen, [1] the main distinction drawn by Maimonides is between laws of Sinaitic origin and other laws, he subdivides the non-Sinaitic laws in a detailed classification, into three groups, as follows :

1. Laws based on *Drash* and Logic
2. *Gezerot*
3. *Takkanot* [2]

This chapter deals with laws based on *drash* and logic only. We shall first give some examples of laws based on logic. We shall then define *"drash"* and give some examples of laws based on *drash*. These laws will be distinguished from laws based on tradition where the *drash* serves as a mere mnemonic. Finally, we shall consider the binding force of laws based upon *drash* and logic and explain the distinction between these laws and *Gezerot* and *Takkanot*.

---

1   p. 33 *ante.*
2   The classification of the Oral Law by Maimonides has *Halachic* significance. From the point of view of *Halachah*, laws in any one group are different from laws in any other group. See Introduction to *Kiryat Sefer* and Kalman Kahane, *Ḥeker Ve-iyun* (Tel-Aviv, 1960) Vol I, p. 32.

SECTION I

LAWS BASED ON LOGIC

Logic in Delegated Legislation

Some questions were specifically delegated to the Sages by the
Torah, so that they should decide them by the use of logic: for
example, what "work" was to be prohibited during the mid-festival
days, [3] and what abnormality in an animal was to make it
trefah, [4] were questions specifically referred to the decision of the
Sages. In such cases, [5] the Sinaitic law merely propounded the principle, that certain works were to be prohibited during the mid-
festival, or that certain abnormalities were to make an animal *trefah*,
and left it to the Sages to work out the details.

Logic in Rabbinic Decisions

There are also instances where the Sages deduced laws by
means of logic, although the problems were not specifically referred to them by the Torah.

For example, the law that one must not kill an innocent man
even in order to save one's own life is based on the logic expressed

---

3   **Hagigah* 18A and see *Bet Yosef, Orah Hayyim* 530 that this is
    d'Oraita contra Tosefot *ad. loc.*, and see **Shney Luhot Habrit, Torah
    Sheb'al Peh.*
4   R. Jonathan Eibushutz, **Kreti, Yore Deah, Trefut* XXIX (5).
5   There are other such cases see N.H.Z. Berlin, *Ha'emek Shelah* 47 (1)
    regarding *Mukzeh;* and **R. Nissim, Yoma* I, 1 regarding washing and
    wearing shoes on Day of Atonement.

in the Talmudic aphorism "who told you that your blood is redder than his?" [6]

The Talmud states that the law which prohibits the carrying of an object from a public domain into a private domain on Sabbath is based on a verse in the Scripture. The carrying of an object in the opposite direction, from a private domain into a public domain, is prohibited on the logical ground that there should be no difference between carrying in one direction and in the other. [7]

Other examples are: the law permitting the use of fruit which was the property of a deceased learned man without first tithing. This was based on the presumption that the fruit is already tithed. The Sages thought it logical that "a learned man will not allow something imperfect to pass out of his possession." [8]

The law requiring a benediction before the eating of food is founded on a logical principle; namely, that one is forbidden to have any benefit from the world without first expressing one's gratitude to God who provided it. [9]

Principles of Law based on Logic

These are only isolated instances of the Sages making law by the use of logic. Some of the basic principles of the law, particularly of the civil law, are founded upon logic. These principles include the presumptions of *Hazakah* [10] and of *Miggo*. [11] They are

6   *Sanhedrin* 74A.
7   *Shabbat* 96B.
8   *Aboda Zara* 41B and *Erubin* 32A.
9   *Berakhot* 35A and see *Pney Yehoshuah, ad. loc.*; R. Ezekiel Landau *Zelah, ad. loc.* states that this does not have *d'Oraita* status, and most commentators agree.
10   Legal presumptions, e.g. that possession indicates ownership (*Baba Mezia* 100A, *Ketubot* 20A); that one does not pay a debt before the due date (*Baba Batra* 5B); that an agent will carry out his instructions (*Erubin* 31B, *Gittin* 64A); that present condition remains unchanged (*Hulin* 9A, *Gittin* III, 3).
11   Presumption that a statement by the witness is true, because had he

among the most important principles of Talmudic jurisprudence
and they have their origin in the interpretation of the intention of
the Torah by means of logic. [12]

SECTION II

LAWS BASED ON DRASH

The Purpose and Nature of Drash

What has been said regarding the nature of laws based on logic
applies equally to the laws based on *drash*. In these laws too, the
Sages were interpreting the intention of the Torah. Here they made
use not of "logic", but of hermaneutic rules which had been
received at Sinai, [1] and perhaps of other rules of language with
which they were familiar. [2] *Drash* is by definition an interpretation
of a Biblical passage. It is, however, an interpretation which is not
in accordance with the plain meaning of the passage. For example,
the Biblical verse "the fathers shall not be put to death on account

intended to lie he could have invented a much more plausible story.
See *Baba Batra* 33A, *Ketubot* II, 3.

12 See Z.H. Chajes, *Mavo Ha-Talmud,* Chapter XV; he also includes
Rov among the principles based on logic. (English translation: *The
Student's Guide through the Talmud,* Feldheim, N.Y. 1969.)

1   Rashi, *Ḥulin* 16A *"Abal"*.
2   See *infra* p. 56 regarding the view of Malbim. R. Judah Halevy,
Kuzari III, 73 writes "they either employed secret methods of interpretation, which we do not know, which were handed down to them,
together with the thirteen *middot* or . . ."

of the children, nor shall the children be put to death on account of the fathers," [3] simply means that the sins of the fathers shall not be visited upon the children and vice versa. [4] By means of *drash*, however, the Sages [5] have derived a rule from this verse that certain relatives are not admissible to give evidence as if "on account of" meant "by the evidence of." Because these interpretations do not follow the plain meaning of Biblical passages, nor the rules of logic, it is important to stress that they follow rules of construction and of language which the Sages had received by way of tradition.

Drash used to connect Laws of Sinaitic origin to the Scripture

It is of even greater importance to appreciate that in many cases what appears as *drash* is not a creation of a new law at all, but a mere connecting of the Oral Law to the Scripture where the law is of Sinaitic origin [6] or has its origin in logic[7] or even is itself of Rabbinic origin.[8] In these cases, the fact that the *drash* is not in accordance with the plain or logical meaning of the texts is of no great significance, because the *drash* itself did not create the laws, but on the contrary, the laws created the *drash*. [9]

---

3   Deut. XXIV, 16.
4   See Nachmanides, Lev. XXVIII, 29.
5   *Sanhedrin* 27B.
6   Maimonides, *Sefer Hamizvot* (Shoresh II), see *infra* p. 71. Also **Introduction to Seder Zera'im.* Also **Or Hahayyim* (R. Hayyim Ibn Attar) Lev. XIII, 34.
7   *Kiddushin* 57B and see Rashi, *ad. loc.* "Rava", also *Shabbat* 135A Tosefot, *ad. loc.* "Velo". **Sanhedrin* 78A. Also *Kitve Maharal of Prague*, (Mossad Harav Kook 1960) Vol. II, p. 284.
8   This subject is discussed at great length by I.I. Halevy, *Dorot Harishonim* I, 5 p. 467 *et seq.*
9   The correct term for *drash* which is not "creative" is *"Asmakhta"*, although as in this chapter, the term *drash* is sometimes used to cover both creative *drash* and *Asmakhta.*

Frequently, it is difficult to ascertain from the Talmud whether a particular *drash is* "creative" or not, in the sense mentioned.[10] In some cases, however, it is self evident that the *drash* is not creative and came after, rather than produced, the law. The case of the *etrog* may serve as an example. The Torah states "But on the fifteenth day of the seventh month ... ye shall take on the first day the fruit of a goodly tree." [11] The Talmud [12] "deduces" by means of a *drash* that "a goodly tree" is an *"etrog* tree." However, it is obvious that this law was known long before the *drash* was ever made. How otherwise was the law fulfilled throughout the centuries that had passed between the giving of the Torah at Sinai and the Talmudic era? Evidently, therefore, this is an example of *drash* being used to connect a Sinaitic law to Scripture, and not in order to produce a new law.

Similarly, the Talmud [13] "deduced" by means of *drash* that for the purpose of ritual slaughter (*Shehitah*) the animal's throat has to be cut. The Talmud [14] also "deduced" by means of *drash* that *Tefillin* must contain four scrolls. These are among the many, examples of laws which are clearly of Sinaitic origin and where the *drash* serves no other purpose than to connect well-established law to Scripture. [15]

---

10 For example, *Yebamot* VIII, 3 quoted at p. 44 *ante*. In some cases, the Talmud, however, states expressly that a *drash* is *Asmakhta* and that the law is of Sinaitic origin: see *Erubin* 4B, *Sukkah* 28A, *Pesahim* 81B, *Ta'anit* 17B, *Niddah* 32A. See also *Hagigah* 4A and *Yebamot* 21A where the Talmud expressly states that a *drash* is *Asmakhta* and that the law is of Rabbinic origin.

11 Lev. XXIII, 39, 40.

12 *Sukkah* 35B.

13 *Hulin* 27A.

14 *Sanhedrin* 4B.

15 See generally, Z.H. Chajes, *Mavo Ha-Talmud*, Chapt. I.

Drash used to connect Laws of Rabbinic origin to the Scripture

A *Baal Keri* (one who has seminal issue) is forbidden to study the Torah. In reply to the question "whence do we know that a *Baal Keri* is forbidden to study the Torah?" the Talmud in *Massekhet Berakhot* [16] produces a *drash* based on Scripture. Yet the law that a *Baal Keri* must not study Torah is one of the *Takkanot* of Ezra [17] and not, in fact, a law based on the Torah.

A place of idol worship is ritually unclean. An entire page of Talmud [18] is devoted to a discussion as to why the law declaring such a place ritually unclean is derived from one verse in the Bible in preference to another. Yet on the following page, the Talmud states that the uncleanness attached to a place of idol worship is the result of a Rabbinic decree.

The Purpose of Drash where it did not "create" Laws

All these cases are instances of *drash* produced by laws; the *drash* was created because the laws were there. Many theories have been advanced to explain the purpose which such *drash* was intended to serve. It has been argued that where the law concerned is of Sinaitic origin, the purpose of *drash* was to show that the oral tradition is contained in the Written Law. [19] It has also been sug-

---

16   **Berakhot* 21B.
17   **Baba Kama* 82A.
18   *Shabbat* 82B.
19   Or *Haḥayyim, ante* Note 6, *Ritva, *Rosh Hashanah* 16A. *Shney Luḥot Habrit (Shloh)* suggests in *Massekhet Shebuot* that the purpose of *Asmakhta* was to show that "there is nothing which the Sages have said which is not indicated in the Torah." (See *Hagoh Beinyan Remez.*) See also Maimonides, *Guide For the Perplexed* III, 43 "They use the text of the Bible as a kind of poetical language, and do not intend thereby to give an interpretation of the text."

gested that at a time when it was not permitted to commit the
Oral Law to writing, *drash* served as a mnemonic to facilitate the
process of memorising. [20] Where the law concerned is of Rabbinic
origin, it has been said that although the *drash* did not directly
produce the law it served as an indication to the Sages that an
enactment of the law concerned is appropriate. [21]

Controversy between Malbim and Halevy

There is, of course, a type of *drash* which actually produced
laws, that is, a *drash* which arose where a point of law was in
question and the Sages turned to the Scripture in order to procure
an answer by means of *drash*. In fact, the Bible commentator,
Malbim (19th Century) suggests [22] that most of the *drash* in the

20   "They connected the *Miẓvah* to the Scripture as a sign that it be known
and remembered" (Maimonides, *Introduction to Seder Zeraim*) "or
they used the verse as an *Asmakhta* or a sign for the tradition they had
received ... they connected them to a verse as an aid to memory"
(Judah Halevy, *Kuzari* III, 73), see also Tosefot, *Menaḥot* 92B
"Girse". If the latter purpose was intended, we think that this will
explain why some *drash* was considered acceptable, although it appears
to be far removed from the plain meaning of the Scripture; if its
purpose was to serve as an aid to memory, then the most extra-ordinary
drash will be the most effective. Joshua Heller, *Maoz Hadat* (Jerusalem, 1965) p. 12, argues that *drash* can be treated as a mnemonic only
in cases where the law is of Rabbinic origin.

21   Ritva, *Rosh Hashanah*, 16A. Also Maharal of Prague, **Gur Arye,
Yitro*. See S.B. Sofer, *Divrey Sofrim*, p. 8, that this argument is con-
fined to laws of Rabbinic origin. A completely different purpose for
Asmakhta is that suggested by Maharal (*Likutim*) namely that laws of
Rabbinic origin were connected to the scripture to invest them with
greater authority. A somewhat different argument is put forward by
Shlo, who suggests that *Asmakhta* indicates that the idea underlying the
relevant passage in the scripture on which the *Asmakhta* is based caused
the sages to enact the relevant law. (See *Torah Sheb'al Peh "Klal"
Rabanan*). See also Rashi, *Berakhot* 20B *"Kideashkeḥan"* which it is
suggested, contains the same idea.

22   **Ayelet Hashaḥar*, Introduction to Leviticus.

Talmud is of this type. He explains that the Sages in their *drash* followed special rules of language which were known to them. These rules of language have been long forgotten and Malbim claims to have re-discovered them. [23]

I.I. Halevy, the Talmudist and historian, is of a different opinion. [24] He considers that *drash* of this type was very rare and that in any event there were no such rules of language as Malbim imagines. Mostly, when a point of law was in doubt the Sages did not use creative *drash* at all. Generally, *drash* was used only after the Sages had already decided the law, having based their decision on tradition and logic. [25]

---

23 He lays down 613 rules which he claims were received by the *Tannaim* for the purpose of interpreting the Hebrew language. The following is an example of one such rule, chosen at random. Rule 166 says: If there are two subjects to a verb; it must be in the plural, unless one of the subjects is the more active or the more important. He then goes on to examine the following text in the light of this rule: "This is the offering of Aaron and his sons which they shall bring near (*Yakrivu*) to God," (Lev. VI, 13). This verse has two subjects — "Aaron" and "his sons"; and a verb in the plural *"Yakrivu"*. According to the rule stated, this means that neither one of the subjects is more active or important than the other. Now we can see that the following drash which appears in the Sifra flows from our rule. The Sifra says: "I would have thought that Aaron and his sons bring one sacrifice between them. But the Scripture says "his sons who sacrifice" (*Yakrivu*). How can this be done? Aaron brings his own offering and his sons bring their own." In other words, the equality indicated by the verb in plural is achieved by each bringing separate offerings. If a joint offering were brought Aaron the High Priest would have taken the major part in the proceeding.

24 *Dorot Harishonim*, Vol. I, 5, p. 487 *et. seq.* and see also *Gur Arye, Yitro*.

25 To the question "why does the Talmud so fiercely debate the validity of a particular scriptural proof if, in fact, the scriptural proof is only an *Asmakhta*?" Halevy provides no satisfactory answer. However, he points to the examples of laws of Rabbinic origin which are treated in the Talmud as derived by *drash*. In these cases, the *drash* is clearly no more than *Asmakhta*, yet the validity of the *drash* is frequently contested and fiercely argued.

SECTION III

THE OBLIGATION TO OBSERVE LAWS DERIVED
BY MEANS OF DRASH AND LOGIC

The obligation to observe the laws of the Torah in general arises out of a covenant between God and Israel "And the Lord said unto Moses 'Write thou these words for after the tenor of these words I have made a covenant with thee and with Israel.' " [1] The Talmud states that the Israelites at first entered into this covenant under coercion, but eventually ratified it voluntarily after the great wonder which they witnessed in the days of Aḥaseurus. [2]

Scriptural Authority for Rabbinic Interpretation

This covenant relates to the Torah which the Israelites received at Sinai and consequently, also to the interpretation of the Torah by the Sages since the Torah clothes this interpretation with authority.[3] "If there be any matter too hard for thee in judgment ... and thou shalt come unto the Priest the Levite and the Judge that shall be in those days and inquire ... and thou shalt observe to do according to all that they inform thee." [4]

The duty to observe the laws derived by means of *drash* and logic is, accordingly, based upon the Torah (or *d'Oraita*) [5] in con-

1   Exod. XXXIV, 27.
2   *Shabbat* 88A.
3   See Nachmanides, *Sefer Hamiẓvot, Shoresh* II. However, it must be noted that laws based on *drash* are in some respects treated less severely than laws expressly stated in the Torah. Tosefot, *Yebamot* 7B "VeOmar"; Ran *Nedarim* 8A; Tosefot-Yom-Tov, *Zebaḥim* X, 2.
4   Deut. VII, 8 and 9.
5   See I. I. Halevy, *op. cit.* I, 5 p. 525, who states that while these interpretations are *d'Oraita*, they are yet liable to be reversed by a later *Bet Din* who consider the logic or *drash* to have been mistaken. See also Maharal of Prague, *Gur Aryeh, Yitro.*

tradistinction to the duty to observe laws newly created by the Sages, which have a lower status (of *d'Rabanan*) and which, generally speaking, may be treated more leniently. [6]

d'Oraita and d'Rabanan Distinguished

This distinction is emphasised most clearly in a case where a person is in doubt whether he has already discharged his obligation regarding a *Mizvah*. If the obligation is *d'Oraita*, he must take the stricter view; if it is *d'Rabanan*, he may take the more lenient view. For example, if the question arises "Is it Sabbath today or Sunday?" or "Has Grace after Meals been recited?" a doubt has been raised concerning *d'Oraita* laws, and consequently the stricter view must be taken. Sabbath must be observed, although one is on a deserted island and not sure which day of the week it is; Grace after Meals has to be recited, although this may already have been done. However, where the doubt is "Were hands properly washed (*netilat yadayim*) before eating bread?" one need not wash one's hands again because the obligation is *d'Rabanan* [7].

---

6   Sometimes the Sages ruled that their laws must be treated as severely or even more severely than Torah laws: *Gittin* 65A, *Erubin* 77A, *Ketubot* IV, 1.

7   *Berakhot* 21A. Rabbinic laws are also treated more leniently inter alia for the following purposes:
   a.   *Pesaḥim* 4B. A woman's evidence is admissible concerning a Rabbinic prohibition even in a case where she has an "Interest" (e.g. to save herself trouble).
   b.   *Ketubot* 28A. Evidence is admissible by a witness of what he saw during his minority where a Rabbinic law is concerned.
   c.   *Shebuot* 23B. On oath not to comply with a Rabbinic decree is valid.

Interpretative Laws have d'Oraita Status

There is definite Talmudic authority for the proposition that laws derived by logic have *d'Oraita* status. On occasions, when in the Talmud one of the Sages quotes from the Scripture to support a certain law, he is met with the objection "why quote from the Scripture? — it is logical! " [8] These statements show clearly that in the view of the Talmud, logic carries the same weight as the Scripture itself.

No such clear Talmudic authority can be found for laws derived by *drash*.[9] The most that can be said is that generally such laws are treated by the authorities as of equal status with *d'Oraita* laws. For example, a woman who was "acquired" (in marriage) by "money" is treated as having *d'Oraita* marital status, although the law that a "woman may be acquired by money" is derived by means of a Talmudic *drash*.[10]

In this connection, however, reference has to be made to a famous dispute between Maimonides and the 12th century Gerona Talmudist and exegete, Nachmanides. Maimonides appears to be taking up a position contrary to what has been stated, namely, to be saying that laws derived by *drash* normally have no higher status than Rabbinic law.

---

8   *Baba Kama* 46B.
9   Although there is no clear Talmudic authority for the proposition that such laws have *d'Oraita* status, there is a hint of this in *Pesaḥim* 18B. In connection with the drash *Kal Va-Ḥomer* (*de minore ad majus*) the Talmud states "although the law might have been deduced by *Kal Va-Ḥomer* yet the Scripture states it expressly." See also *Nazir* 47B, *Kiddushin* 4B. See also in connection with *Mah Maẓinu*, *Zebaḥim* 49B. See also *Berakhot* 20B where a law deduced by *Hekesh* is called "from the Torah."
10   *Kiddushin* I, 1 and 3B.

Controversy between Maimonides and Nachmanides

In his *Sefer Hamizvot*, [11] Maimonides enumerates the *Mizvot* of the Torah. According to a view expressed in the Talmud, [12] the number of such *Mizvot* is six hundred and thirteen. [13] In order to arrive at this traditional number, Maimonides excludes several of the enactments of the Torah. For example, he excludes *Mizvot* which applied only during a limited period of time, [14] and also *Mizvot* which are of a general nature and which do not require specific action to be taken. [15] He also excludes *Mizvot* which are derived by *drash* and, in this connection he makes the statement that such *Mizvot* must be presumed to be *d'Rabanan* where the contrary is not stated.

However, this statement cannot be accepted as final. Firstly, it is severely criticised by Nachmanides, [16] who states that such laws must be presumed to be *d'Oraita* in the absence of contrary evidence. Secondly, various commentators point out that Maimonides classified a number of laws derived by *drash* as being *d'Oraita*.

11 *Shoresh* II.

12 *Makkot* 23.

13 See Introduction to *Kiryat Sefer* (Mabit) for the legal consequences which flow from the fact that a law is *d'Oraita* and (i) of the Oral Law but not of the Written Law, (ii) of the Written Law, but not counted as one of the six hundred and thirteen *Mizvot*.

14 For instance, the prohibition against leaving manna from one morning to the next, which only applied during the time when the Israelites sojourned in the desert (Exod. XVI, 19).

15 For instance, the commandment "in all that I have said unto you take heed" (Exod. XXIII, 13).

16 *ad. loc.*

Maimonides Explained

The suggestion has been made that the original Arabic text of *Sefer Hamizvot* has been mis-translated. That Maimonides had not said that such laws have *d'Rabanan* status, but that laws derived by *drash* are *Divrey Sofrim*. In the terminology of Maimonides, the expression *"Divrey Sofrim"* includes all laws which are not expressly stated in the Scripture, [17] whether they have *d'Oraita* status or not. In that view, Maimonides would agree that laws derived by *drash* which are *Divrey Sofrim* have *d'Oraita* status in every respect. [18]

The Status of Rabbinic Laws varies according to whether the Sages were 'Legislating' or 'Interpreting'

If laws derived by means of *drash* and logic have the status of *d'Oraita*, notwithstanding that they are not of Sinaitic origin, why have *Gezerot* and *Takkanot* the inferior status of *d'Rabanan*? The answer appears to be that whereas the Sages have a function in producing both types of law, their function is different in each case. The Sages produced laws derived by *drash* and logic as *interpreters* of Sinaitic law. They produced *Gezerot* and *Takkanot* as *legislators*. For example, when the Sages stated that it is prohi-

---

17 *Kinat Sofrim, ad. loc.* See Maimonides definition of *Divrey Sofrim* on *Kelim* XVII, 12 and *Mikvaot* VII, 7.

18 **Megillat Esther ad. loc.* He also suggests that Maimonides is not at all concerned in distinguishing between *d'Oraita* and *d'Rabanan*, but between laws which can be *counted* among "the 613" and those which cannot. *Lev Sameah* suggests that Maimonides accords *d'Oraita* status to laws derived by *drash* only where the *drash* concerns a detail of a law which is in itself *d'Oraita*, e.g. the principle of *Kiddushin* is *d'Oraita*, therefore the drash enabling *Kiddushin* by "money" is also *d'Oraita*.

bited to kill an innocent man even in order to save one's own life, [19] they were interpreting the Sinaitic law "Thou shalt not kill." [20] Similarly, in other cases they were interpreting the intention of the Torah in a general sense, even if they were not interpreting a specific scriptural law. In laws based on logic they were in fact saying "this law is so obvious that the Torah must have intended it."

On the other hand, when the Sages stated the law of *Mukzeh* [21] they were *creating* new law; they had the tradition that only thirty-nine types of "work" were prohibited on Sabbath, [22] and therefore "thou shalt do no work" [23] could not be interpreted to include the prohibition of *Mukzeh*. This is an instance of new law being made by the Sages. Wherever the Sages acted as *interpreters* they did not actually *make* the law and the law is therefore *d'Oraita;* wherever they acted as legislators they *made* the law and the law they produced is *d'Rabanan*.[24]

---

19 *ante* p. 50.
20 Exod. XX, 13.
21 This law prohibits the handling of objects on Sabbath which one would not expect to use that day e.g. because the object only came into being on Sabbath, or because it is repulsive, or because it is altogether too valuable for use, or because it serves a purpose which is inappropriate for Sabbath e.g. to make fire.
22 *Shabbat* 73A.
23 Exod. XX, 10.
24 For the distinction between interpretive laws and others, see also *Sermons of Ran* (Sermon 7), and Prof. M. Elon, *Israel Law Review,* Vol. IX, No. 4, p. 542 *et. seq.*

HEBREW SOURCES

SECTION I

QUESTIONS OF LAW SPECIFICALLY DELEGATED TO THE SAGES

3. *Ḥagigah 18A*

תניא אידך : "ששת ימים תאכל מצות וביום השביעי עצרת לה'" מה שביעי
עצור אף ששת ימים עצורין. אי מה שביעי עצור בכל מלאכה אף ששת ימים
עצורין בכל מלאכה תלמוד לומר "וביום השביעי עצרת" השביעי עצור בכל
מלאכה ואין ששה ימים עצורין בכל מלאכה. הא לא מסרן הכתוב אלא לחכמים
לומר לך אי זה יום אסור ואי זה יום מותר אי זו מלאכה אסורה ואי זו מלאכה
מותרת.

3. *Shney Luḥot Habrith, Torah Sheb'al-Peh, Klal Rabanan*

ד' עניינים הם מישך שייכי בדרבנן : א. היא דרבנן והיא מדאורייתא שהתורה
נתנה ביד החכמים כמ"ש מקצת הפוסקים בענין מלאכת חול המועד שהוא
מדאורייתא אלא שהתורה מסרה לחכמים שיאסרו המלאכות שנראה להם
ויתירו מה שנראה להם.

4. *Kreti, Yoreh Deah, Trefut XXIX, 1.5*

שמונה מיני טריפות הן. דרוסה נקובה וכו' : בגמרא נאמר הלכה למשה
מסיני הם... שנגמסרו כך דרך כלל טריפות נקובה וכו' וחז"ל כפי חכמתם
ועוצם בינתם בפלפל התורה וכדומה בררו ענין כלל הוא איך יסתעף הימנה
פרטיה.

5. R. Nisim, *Yoma* I, 1

ובגמרא נמי אמרינן דמי שיש לו חטטים בראשו סך כדרכו ואינו חושש
ומי שידיו מלוכלכות בטיט ובצואה רוחץ כדרכו ואינו חושש ואי סיכה ורחיצה
דאורייתא נינהו היכי מקילינן בהו הכי אלא ודאי מדרבנן נינהו והיינו נמי
דאמרינן בגמ' "הני חמישה ענויין כנגד מי?" ומדאמרינן כנגד מי ולא אמרינן
מנא לן משמע דמדרבנן נינהו ולא בעי אלא אם יש להם שום רמז מן התורה —
כך העלו בתוספות: וקשיא לי מדתני' בגמ'" אף על פי שאמרו אסור לא אמרו
עונש כרת אלא על האוכל ועל השותה ועושה מלאכה בלבד" ואם איתא דהני
ענויי אחריני מדרבנן בעלמא נינהו היכי שייך למימר בהו "ולא אמרו עונש
כרת" דהא אפי' איסורא דאורייתא נמי ליכא. לפיכך היה נראה לי דכולהו
מדאורייתא נינהו אלא דכיון דלאו בכלל ענויי דכתיבי בקרא בהדיא באורייתא
נינהו אלא מריבויא דשבתון אתו וכדאיתא בגמרא קילי טפי ומסרן הכתוב
לחכמים והן הקלו בהן כפי מה שראו והתירו כל שאינו נעשה לתענוג.

LAWS DEDUCED BY "LOGIC"

6. *Sanhedrin* 74A

רוצח גופיה מנא לן? סברא הוא דההוא דאתא לקמיה דרבה ואמר ליה
אמר לי מרי דוראי (רש"י — אדון עירי ונכרי הוה) זיל קטליה לפלניא ואי
לא קטלינא לך אמר ליה לקטלוך ולא תקטול — מי יימר לך דדמא דידך סומק
טפי — דילמא דמא דהוא גברא סומק טפי.

7. *Shabbat* 96B

אשכחן הוצאה, הכנסה מנלן סברא היא מרשות לרשות הוא מה לי אפוקי
ומה לי עיולי.

8. *Aboda Zara* 41B

חבר שמת והניח מגורה מלאה פירות אפילו הן בני יומן הרי הן בחזקת
מתוקנין ... חזקה על חבר שאינו מוציא דבר שאינו מתוקן מתחת ידו.

9. *Berakhot* 35A

כיצד מברכין על הפירות וכו'. מנא ה"מ? ... סברא הוא אסור לו לאדם
שיהנה מן העולם הזה בלא ברכה.

SECTION II

DRASH WHERE THE LAW IS OF SINAITIC ORIGIN

6. Maimonides, *Introduction to Seder Zeraim*

שהפרושים המקבלים מפי משה — אין מחלקת בהם בשום פנים.

שהרי מאז ועד עתה לא מצאנו מחלקת שנפלה בזמן מן הזמנים... במה
שאמר הכתוב "פרי עץ הדר" כדי שיאמר אחד שהוא אתרוג; ויאמר אחר
שהוא חבושים או רמונים... וכיוצא בהן בכלל המצוות אין מחלוקת בהן
שכולן פרושים מקובלים מפי משה, ועליהם ועל דומיהם אמרו "כל התורה
נאמרו כללותיה ופרטותיה ודקדוקיה מסיני" אבל אף על פי שהם מקובלים
ואין מחלוקת בהם — הרי היא מחכמת התורה הנתונה לנו, שנוכל להוציא
ממנה אלו הפירושים בדרך מדרכי הסברות, והאסמכתות והראיות והרמזים
המצויים במקרא — וכשתראה אותם בתלמוד מעיינים וחולקים זה על זה
במערכת העיון ומביאין ראיות על אחד מאלו הפרושים והדומה להם, כגון
מה שאמרו במאמר "פרי עץ הדר" אולי יהיה רמונים או חבושים או זולתם
עד שהביאו ראיה עליו ממה שנאמר "פרי עץ הדר" ואמרו "עץ שטעם עצו
ופריו שוין" ואמר אחר "פרי הדר באילנות משנה לשנה" ואמר אחר "פרי
הדר על כל מים" — אלו הראיות לא הביאון מפני שנשתבש עליהם העניין
עד שנודע להם מהראיות האלה; אבל ראינו בלא ספק מיהושע עד עתה
שהאתרוג היו לוקחים עם הלולב בכל שנה ואין בו מחלוקת אבל חקרו על
הרמז הנמצא בכתוב לזה הפרוש המקובל.

6. *Or Haḥayyim*, Lev. XIII, 34

וראיתי ליישב מאמרי ז"ל שאמרו שלא היה דבר שלא נמסר למשה בסיני
ואפילו מה שתלמיד ותיק עתיד לחדש. ואמרו במקום אחר כי רבי עקיבא
הי' דורש מה שלא ידע משה. כאומר הדברים עשיתים אעשה לא נאמר וכו'
יעש"ד. וכן כמה מאמרים שדומים לזה. ונראה כי ישוב המאמרים הוא כי
הן אמת שכל דבר תורה נאמ' למשה ואין חכם יכול לדעת יותר ממה שידע
משה. והגם שתצטרף כל דורות ישראל מיום מתן תורה עד שתמלא הארץ דעה
אין חידוש שלא ידע משה. אבל ההפרש הוא כי משה נתן לו ה' תורה שבכתב
ותורה שבעל פה. והנ' האדון ב"ה בחכמתו ית' רשם בתורה שבכתב כל התורה
שבעל פה שאמר למשה אבל לא הודיע למשה כל מה שנתן לו בע"פ היכן
רמוז בתורה שבכתב. וזו היא עבודת בני ישראל עמלי תורה שייישבו ההלכות

שנאמרו למשה בסיני והסודות והדרשות כלן יתנו להם מקום בתורה שבכתב.
ולזה תמצא באומ' התנאים וחברו ת״כ וספרי וכו' וכל דרשותם בכתובים
אינם אלא ע״פ ההלכות. והלבישו' בתורת ה' תמימה שבכתב ואחריה'. ועד
היום זו היא עבודת הקודש בני תורה לדייק המקראות ולייש ע״פ המאמרים
שהם תורה שבעל פה. וזו היא עבוד' התורה הנקראת ארץ החיים. וענין זה
לא נמסר למשה כולו לדעת כל תורה שבעל פה היכן היא כולה רמוזה בתורה
שבכתב. ולזה אמרו ז״ל שדרש ר״ע דרשות שלא ידעם משה, אין הכוונה
שלא ידע משה עקרן של דברים, הלא ממנו הכל אפי' מה שתלמיד ותיק עתיד
לחדש. אלא שלא ידע סמיכתם ודיוקם היכן רמוזים בתורה. וזה לך האות מה
שלפנינו, שדרש הלל מהכתוב ההלכה שנאמרה למשה בעל פה ולא גילה ה'
למשה עקרה בכתוב, ובא הלל ודרשה. ודברים אלו נכונים הם.

DRASH WHERE THE LAW IS BASED ON LOGIC

7. *Sanhedrin* 78A

תנו רבנן הכוהו עשרה בני אדם בעשרה מקלות ומת בין בבת־אחת בין
בזה אחר זה פטורין. ר' יהודה בן בתירא אומר בזה אחר זה האחרון חייב
מפני שקירב את מיתתו. אמר ר' יוחנן ושניהם מקרא אחד דרשו "ואיש כי
יכה כל נפש אדם" רבנן סברי כל נפש וכו'... ור' יהודה בן בתירא סבר
כל נפש וכו'... אמר רבא הכל מודים בהורג את הטריפה שהוא פטור בגוסס
בידי שמים שהוא חייב לא נחלקו אלא בגוסס בידי אדם מר מדמי ליה לטרפה
ומר מדמי ליה לגוסס.

DRASH WHERE THE LAW IS OF RABBINIC ORIGIN

16. *Berakhot* 21B

מנין לבעל קרי שאסור בדברי תורה שנאמר "והודעתם לבניך ולבני בניך"
וסמיך ליה "יום אשר עמדת וגו'" מה להלן בעלי קריין אסורין אף כאן בעלי
קריין אסורין וכי תימא ר״י לא דריש סמוכים וכו'.

17. *Baba Kama* 82A

עשרה תקנות תיקן עזרא... ותיקן טבילה לבעלי קריין.

SCRIPTURE INDICATES THAT AN ENACTMENT OF A LAW
BY THE SAGES IS APPROPRIATE

19.   Ritva, *Rosh Hashanah 16A*

שכל מה שיש לו אסמכתא מן הפסוק העיר הקב"ה שראוי לעשות כן אלא
שלא קבעו חובה ומסרו לחכמים. וזה דבר ברור ואמת ולא כדברי המפרשים
האסמכתאות שהוא כדרך סמן שנתנו חכמים ולא שכונת התורה לכך ח"ו
ישתקע הדבר ולא יאמר שזו דעת מינות הוא אבל התורה העירה בכך ומסרו
חיוב הדבר לקבעו חכמים אם ירצו כמ"ש ועשית ע"פ הדבר אשר יגידו לך
ולפיכך תמצא החכמים נותנים בכל מקום ראיה או זכר או אסמכתא לדבריהם
מן התורה כלומר שאינם מחדשים דבר מלבם וכל תורה שבע"פ רמוזה בתורה
שהיא תמימה וח"ו שהיא חסירה כלום.

21.   Maharal of Prague, *Gur Aryeh, Yitro*

ואל תטעה לומר, כי בכל מקום שאמרו ז"ל אסמכתא היא, שמשה רבנו כאשר
כתב התורה לא כתב אותו בשביל אותה אסמכתא, רק הם ז"ל אסמכוה אותה
מדעתם. אומר אני, האומר כן טועה בדברי חכמים, שאם כן יהיו דברי חכמים
רק עמל ויגיעה ואין בו ממש, שלפעמים מוציאים דבר מן המקרא על ידי
לימוד דרשות ולא יהיה זה רק ליפות הדברים או לגנוב דעת הבריות כאילו
היא דרשה מן התורה, ולא נאה זה לחכם, שהרי אין להם שום חלק ונחלה
בתורה אלא הם ז"ל אסמכוה אותה מדעתם אקרא. אבל כך פירושו שיש
לדבריהם אסמכתא — שדבריהם נסמכים אקרא, ונקרא זה אסמכתא, כלומר
שאין זה גוף המקרא אלא שנסמכים דבריהם על דברי תורה ומחוברים אל
דברי התורה, ולעולם בתורה יש להם חלק. והשתא כל הדרשות שדרשו חכמים
ז"ל הם שפיר לסמוך דבריהם על הכתוב. לפעמים הוא פירוש הכתוב, כמו
גבי תפילין שעיקרו מדברי תורה ופירושו מדברי סופרים, ואין זה אסמכתא
אלא פירוש דברי תורה, וכן הרבה למאד. כי מאחר שהדרשה בעצמה חכמים
דרשוה נקרא זה דברי סופרים כל דבר הבא מדעתם ושכלם, וזה הדבר יש לו
דין דברי תורה, אבל לפעמים אין הגוף דברי תורה רק נסמך לדברי תורה
ומצטרף על דברי תורה, וכיון דלא הוי רק שנסמך על דברי תורה יש לו דין אחר,
דהוי מדרבנן לגמרי. כי נראה לי כל הדרשות שדרשו חכמים כולן הן מן התורה,
ולא שהן גוף התורה רק הן יוצאות מן התורה. דמיון זה הבנאי בונה בית
והניח מקום להעמיד שם דברים הצריכים אל הבית, ובא אחר כך חכם אחד
ומתבונן בבית, למה בנה הבית בצורה זאת — רק להוסיף דבר זה, ועוד בנאו

בצורה זאת להוסיף דבר זה. הנה כל התוספות הוסיף האיש החכם, אבל
הוא לקח אותם מבנין הבית, ולפעמים החכם מבאר ומפרש איזה דבר נקרא
בית ואיזה חדר, ואין זה תוספות רק פירוש וביאור. כך התורה ניתנה בלא
תוספות בלא מגרעת, והניחה לחכמים מקום, והם הרמזים בתורה ומכל מקום
מאחר שלא כתב זאת בפירוש כאילו אמרה תורה: אתם החכמים יש לכם
במקום הזה להוסיף והיא דעתכם. אבל אין כל כך דבר הכרחי כמו דעת
בתורה, שזה החילוק בין הדברים שהם אסמכתא, שאין כל כך הכרחי כמו
דברי תורה. אך עתה עמדו דרשנים דורשים דברים אשר לא כן כל העולה על
רוחם ודעתם, ואין ספק אלי שההתורה חוגרת שק עליהם, לפרש התורה כרצונם.
וזהו מעשה האומות שמפרשים כרצונם ובזה האמת נעדרת תחת אשר נקראת
תורת אמת.

THE SAGES FOLLOWED SPECIAL RULES OF LANGUAGE
WHICH WERE KNOWN TO THEM

22.	Malbim, *Ayelet Hashaḥar, Introduction to Leviticus*

על זאת נשמו אחרונים וקדמונים התפלאו, לאמר זאת התורה אשר לנו
הנקראת בשם תורה שבע"פ מה יסודה...

כי כל מעיין... יראה שהיא נסמכת תמיד על משענת הכתובים ונדרשת מן
המקראות... אולם כאשר נבקר את הכתובים עצמם... נראה שלא לבד
שאין פשט המקרא מכריח את הדרוש ההוא שהוציאו ממנו כי גם לפעמים
היה בהפך...

וכאשר שאלנו לדור ראשון ומזקנים נתבונן מה ענו על זאת, ראינו כי מלבם
יוציאו מלים שהכתובים המובאים לראיה אל ההלכות הם רק ציונים ואסמכתות
אשר הציבו להם ציונים לעורר הזכרון. ועקרי ההלכות היו מקובלות בידם בעל
פה וזה רחוק מאד... ...חיבורי הנוכחי... הוא ילחם את אויבי הקבלה
בשער... ובא בו האות והמופת כי תורת הפה היא התורה שנתנה מן השמים
וכי כל דברי תורה שבע"פ מוכרחים ומוטבעים בפשט הכתוב ובעומק הלשון. וכי
הדרוש הוא לבדו הוא הפשט הפשוט המיוסד כפי חוקי הלשון האמיתיים
והברורים. וכל מקום אשר דרשו חז"ל איזה דרוש יש שם איזה זר היוצא
מכללי הלשון. וע"י הדרוש ישוב הכתוב לאיתנו כמשפט הלשון וחקותיו.
וכל דרש אשר דרשו אינו בודד במקום ההוא לבדו רק כן דרשו וכן פירשו
בכ"מ אשר בא הזרות הזה.

THE SAGES DID NOT USE "CREATIVE" *DRASH* AT ALL

24.   I. I. Halevy, *Dorot Harishonim,* Vol. I, 5 p. 487

והלא הדבר הזה לבדו די להכריע ולברר את כל הדבר כמו שהוא. שכל
הדרשות בדרכי הדרשות השתמשו בהם רק או לסמוך את הקבלה הידועה
והחלוטה בדרך של ליכא מידי דלא רמיזי בקרא, או גם לתמוך את דבריהם
במקום שהחליטו והכריעו כן מתוך יסודי המשנה או מתוך קבלתם מרבותיהם
או מתוך הסברא מתוך ידיעת יסודי התורה. אבל לא להכריע במקום שהיה
להם ספק, וכשלא יכלו להכריע הדבר מתוך יסודי הקבלה או מסברה גמורה
של דרכי התורה.

SECTION III

LAWS DERIVED BY *DRASH* NORMALLY HAVE
D'RABANAN STATUS

11.   *Maimonides, Sefer Hamiẓvot, Shoresh Sheni*

השרש השני שאין ראוי למנות כל מה שלמדים באחת משלש עשרה מדות
שהתורה נדרשת בהן או מרבוי :

כבר בארנו בפתיחת חבורנו בפירוש המשנה שרוב דיני התורה יצאו בשלש
עשרה מדות ... הנה פעמים תפול בו המחלוקת ושיש שם דינין הן פירושים
מקובלים ממשה אין מחלוקת בהם אבל הם מביאין ראיה עליהן באחת משלש
עשרה מידות כי מחכמת הכתוב שהוא אפשר שימצא בו רמז מורה על הפירוש
ההוא המקובל או היקש יורה עליו וכבר בארנו זה הענין שם. וכשיהיה זה
כן הנה לא כל מה שנמצא לחכמים שהוציאו בהיקש משלש עשרה מדות
נאמר שהוא נאמר למשה בסיני ולא גם כן נאמר בכל מה שימצא בתלמוד
שיסמכוהו אל אחת משלש עשרה מדות שהוא דרבנן, כי פעמים יהיה הפירוש
ההוא מקובל ממשה בסיני לפי הראוי בזה שכל מה שלא תמצאהו כתוב בתורה
ותמצאהו בתלמוד שלמדוהו באחת משלש עשרה מדות אם בארו הם בעצמם
ואמרו שזה גוף תורה או שזה דאורייתא הנה ראוי למנותו אחר שהמקובלים
ממנו אמרו שהוא דאורייתא. ואם לא יבארו זה ולא דברו בו הנה הוא דרבנן
שאין שם כתוב יורה עליו.

16.   *Nachmanides ad. loc.*

....ולפי זה הראוי הוא שנאמר בהפך שכל דבר הנדרש בתלמוד באחת
מכל י"ג מידות הוא מדאורייתא עד שנשמע אותם שיאמרו שהוא אסמכתא.

18.   *Megillat Esther ad. loc.*

שגם זו היא כוונת הרב שכל דבר הנלמד בי"ג המדות הוא מן התורה
ודינו כדין הדברים המפורשים בתורה רק שלא יבואו במנין תרי"ג מצוות....
כן הוא כל דבר הנלמד מהמדות אצל רז"ל דין תורה אף על פי שהוא קורא
אותם מד"ס. וכן בפי' המשנה בפ' י"ז במסכת כלים הוא כתב כי מאמר ד"ס
יכלול שיהא הדבר דעת סופרים כמו הפירושים וההלכות המקובלים ממשה
והולכין בספק להחמיר.

CHAPTER III

LAWS CREATED BY RABBINIC LEGISLATION

CHAPTER III

LAWS CREATED BY RABBINIC LEGISLATION

INTRODUCTION

By definition; the origin of Sinaitic Law is certain; on the other hand it is not always certain what purpose the laws were intended to serve, because God's reason for *Mizvot* is not normally revealed. However, they have to be obeyed, because they are God's command.

Takkanot and *Gezerot* — the two types of Rabbinic legislation — are different in this respect. Their date of origin is not always certain nor is it quite clear why we are obliged to observe them. On the other hand it is generally possible to establish the purpose which they were intended to serve. The main problems to be considered in this chapter are when and why the major *Takkanot* and *Gezerot* were enacted, and the nature of the obligation to observe these enactments.

SECTION I

THE AGE OF THE MAJOR RABBINIC ENACTMENTS

Enactments of the Pre-Mishnaic Era

The Talmud reports the authorship of some isolated *Gezerot* and *Takkanot* and goes back as far as Moses to whom it attributes

"Many *Gezerot* and *Takkanot.*" [1] Important decrees are attributed, among others, to Joshua, [2] King David, [3] King Solomon, [4] Ezra, [5] and the Men of the Great Synagogue, to whom we are indebted for the Purim festivities; [6] to Johanan, the High Priest, [7] to Jose b. Joezer [8] and his colleague Jose b. Johanan, and to the *Bet Din* of

1   *Shabbat* 30A. For example, the seven days of marriage festivities and seven days of mourning for the dead (*Jerus. Ketubot* I, 1), the first benediction of Grace after Meals (*Berakhot* 48B) and the obligation to preach and study the laws of a festival during the festival (*Megillah* 32A) are also attributed to Moses.

2   There are ten *Takkanot* ascribed to Joshua in connection with the land of Israel. Such as; that small cattle may pasture in large private woods; that springs emerging for the first time on private land may be used by all the townspeople; that anyone may fish in Lake Tiberias and that paths across private land may be used by the public until the second rain (*Erubin* 17A). Joshua was also said to have instituted the second blessing of the Grace after Meals (*Berakhot* 48B) and to have confirmed a *Gezerah* against intermarriage with *Netinim* (*Yebamot* 79A).

3   King David promulgated a *Gezerah* against *Yihud* with an unmarried woman (*Aboda Zara* 36B) and the third blessing in Grace after Meals is attributed to him (*Berakhot* 48B).

4   Of King Solomon it is said that he instituted the *Erub* which permitted carrying from a private domain into a courtyard after he himself had made the *Gezerah* prohibiting this. He also made a *Gezerah* declaring a person's hands unclean for touching holy things (*Shabbat* 14B).

5   Among the *Gezerot* of Ezra was one depriving Levites of their right to tithe (*Yebamot* 86B). Among his *Takkanot* was one requiring Courts of Law to sit on Mondays and Thursdays (*Baba Kama* 82A) and another *Takkanah* requiring the Torah to be read in public on Sabbath afternoon.

6   The Men of the Great Synagogue were also responsible for the *Amidah*.

7   Johanan, the High Priest, decreed that produce purchased from an *Am Haarez* (unlearned person) must be assumed not to have been tithed. Also that no hammer should strike in Jerusalem on *Hol Hamo'ed* (*Sotah* 48A).

8   Jose b. Joezer of Zereda and Jose b. Johanan of Jerusalem declared unclean all heathen countries and all glass utensils capable of becoming unclean (*Shabbat* 14B).

the Hasmoneans, to whom we owe the Festival of Lights, Hanuk-kah. [9] It will be noted that all these *Gezerot* and *Takkanot* pre-ceded the Mishnaic era, which opened with Hillel and Shammai.

In fact, it is claimed by Halevy [10] that all major *Takkanot* and *Gezerot* had been decreed prior to the era of Hillel and Shammai. Halevy, in developing the argument, relies mainly on the fact that the major Rabbinic decrees are not reported as having been in-stituted by any one particular person, but are reported anony-mously and without dispute.

Anonymous Enactments of the Era of the Sanhedrin

As we have already explained, [11] mostly when non-Sinaitic laws are reported anonymously, this indicates that they date back to the time when the Sanhedrin was in existence. Only when the Sanhedrin had ceased, and there was no forum where disputes could be settled, did *Halachah* become subject to controversies, with the consequence that statements of *Halachah* had to be attri-buted to individual sages and schools. According to Halevy, [12] the many *Takkanot* and *Gezerot* which appear anonymously and un-disputed, are therefore likely to date back to the time of the San-hedrin. Since, in fact, with very few exceptions, most major Rabbi-nic decrees are expressed anonymously and without controversy, it is reasonable to assume that by the time the Sanhedrin ceased to function, that is, by the beginning of the *Mishnaic* era, most major *Gezerot* and *Takkanot* were firmly established.

---

9   They also made a *Gezerah* against the teaching of Greek wisdom and the rearing of swine (*Sotah* 49B).

10   *op. cit.* Part I Vol. III, p. 223, and see also p. 311 *et. seq.*

11   *ante* p. 32.

12   A similar view is expressed by Z. H. Chajes, *Mavo Ha-Talmud,* p. 58. Translation J. Schachter, (Feldheim, N.Y.)

If in order to take one set of Rabbinic laws as an example, we turn to the Sabbath laws, it will be found that "all the *Gezerot* which the Sages issued in connection with the restriction of work on Sabbath are anonymous." [13] A very impressive list of such *Gezerot* can be produced. They include the prohibition against setting food on a stove lest one might be tempted to stir the fire; [14] a similar prohibition against covering up food with material that generates heat; [15] the prohibition against a woman going into the street wearing specified ornaments, in case she might carry them, in order to show them off to a friend; [16] the prohibition against a non-Jew doing work for a Jew; [17] the prohibition against the administration of justice, the conclusion of a betrothal or the transaction of a loan, lest one should come to write; [18] the prohibition against swimming, lest one should come to repair a swimming-vessel, the prohibition against examining accounts, lest one should come, to make notes, [19] and so on.

Enactments disputed by early Tannaim

Apart from the fact that they are stated anonymously there is another factor which indicates that many Sabbath *Gezerot* are of pre-Talmudic origin. [20] This is the fact that many *Mishnayot* report disputes by the earliest *Tannaim* concerning *details* in the application of such *Gezerot*. These early *Tannaim* argue about the extent of these *Gezerot*, in what type of case they apply and in what

13 Z.H. Chajes, *op. cit.*
14 *Shabbat* III, 1.
15 *ibid.* IV, 1.
16 *ibid.* VI, 1 and 59B.
17 *ibid.* 110A.
18 *Bezah* V, 2.
19 *Shabbat* 150A.
20 See *Halevy, *op. cit.* Vol. I, 3 p. 220 *et seq.* p. 311 *et. seq.*

circumstances they can be considered inapplicable; but even these first *Tannaim* never call in question the existence of the *Gezerot*. It can therefore be safely assumed that the *Gezerot* themselves were of long standing by the beginning of the *Mishnaic* era, otherwise it would have been impossible for the earliest *Tannaim* to have disputes about their details.

The oldest dispute recorded in the *Mishnah*, to which previous reference has been made, [21] may serve as an illustration of what has been stated. This dispute concerned the *Gezerah* of *Mukzeh*, [22] a prohibition which was directed against the handling of animals and other things not suitable for use on Sabbath and *Yom Tov*. Here the *Mishnah* reports how the Sages, generations before the Talmudic era, argued whether this prohibition extended even to a case where the handling of animals was required in order to comply with the ritual prescribed by the Torah for Temple offerings. The Sages, therefore, generations before the *Tannaim,* already knew the principle of *Mukzeh* and their controversy concerned only a detail in its application.

Similarly, early in the *Mishnaic* era there is a dispute recorded in the *Mishnah* [23] between Bet Hillel and Bet Shammai, regarding the type of food which could be set on a stove on Sabbath. In that *Mishnah* too it can be seen that both Bet Hillel and Bet Shammai clearly knew the *Gezerah* against setting food on the stove on Sabbath, and their dispute concerned only the question of how far this *Gezerah* extended.

As a final example, reference may be made to *Bameh Mad-*

---

21 *ante* p. 32 Note 2.
22 *ante* p. 63 Note 21.
23 *Shabbat* III, 1.

likin,[24] the chapter of the *Mishnah,* which in some communities forms part of the regular Friday night service. The various Sages mentioned in that chapter discuss which oils are permitted to be used for Sabbath lights and which are not permitted. This again shows that the principle of the *Takkanah,* that Sabbath lights have to be kindled, was well established beyond all disputes by the time of these *Tannaim,* and that only the *detail,* which oils were to be used, was open to question and doubt.

Rabbinic Enactments in the Mishnaic Era

What has been said of *Gezerot* and *Takkanot* concerning Sabbath laws is typical of Rabbinic laws. They usually appear anonymously and it must be assumed that they had for the most part been concluded by the beginning of the Talmudic era. Nevertheless, there are important exceptions and mention is made in the Talmud of *Gezerot* and *Takkanot* which were decreed by individual *Tannaim* or their schools. For example, the Talmud reports *Gezerot* in the names of Hillel and Shammai and their schools after them. Bet Hillel and Bet Shammai [25] were said to have introduced thirty-six *Gezerot,* on eighteen of which their two schools were agreed, while the remainder followed the view of Bet Shammai only. Joshua b. Gamla "is remembered for good," because he introduced the *Takkanah* of elementary education in all cities, [26] and R. Johanan

---

24 *Shabbat* II, 1 and see Ra'abad, *Sefer Hakabalah.* It may be useful to add here that even where a certain *Takkanah* is stated to be introduced by one of the Sages, it may date back to a much older established custom which the Sage in question merely re-affirmed. See A. Korman, *Mavo L'Torah She-biktab Ve-Sheb'al Peh* (Tel-Aviv, 1966) p. 47 *et. seq.*

25 See *Shabbat* 15A.

26 *Baba Batra* 21A.

b. Zakkai, who after the destruction of the Temple had to guide the people in their tragic circumstances, has to be mentioned for his *Takkanot* and *Gezerot* mainly "as a remembrance of the *Bet Hamikdash.*" [27] So the record of Rabbinic decrees continues with those of R. Eliezer b. Azariah, [28] of R. Gamliel of Yabneh, [29] of the Sages at Usha [30] and of others too numerous to specify. The fact, however, remains that all those *Takkanot* were on matters of detail; the broad basis of Rabbinic legislation had been laid many centuries earlier, long before the time of the Mishnah and the Talmud.

27 He decreed that buildings should not be built and painted like royal palaces, and that one should leave a square ell undecorated over the entrance of any building. He prescribed signs of mourning in connection with a woman's cosmetics, the bridegroom's dress and the setting of a table for meals (*Baba Batra* 60B). Also among the *Takkanot* of Rabbi Joḥanan, was one for blowing the *Shofar*, when Rosh Hashanah coincided with Sabbath, wherever there was a *Bet Din*, and also one that the *Lulab* should be used for seven days during the festival of *Sukkot* (*Rosh Hashanah* 31B).

28 On the day that R. Eliezer b. Azariah was appointed *Nasi*, it was decreed that the Scrolls of Ecclesiastes and the Song of Songs should render hands unclean, thus putting those scrolls on an equal footing with the remainder of the Holy Writ.

29 R. Gamliel of Yabneh invalidated the *Sheḥita* of a Samaritan (*Ḥulin* 5B) and introduced an additional benediction in the *Amidah* (*Nedarim* 28B).

30 Named after one of the meeting places of the Sages in the middle of the second century (*Ketubot* 49B). These include a decree that not more than a fifth of one's income may be given to charity. They also include a number of decrees concerning family law. Such as a provision that parents must support their small children and that a son must support his father in a case where the latter has transferred all his property to him.

SECTION II

THE PURPOSE OF RABBINIC LEGISLATION

Enactments which Experience had shown necessary

The reasons for some *Takkanot* and *Gezerot* are quite apparent, because they were enacted to cure a specific mischief, frequently not hypothetical, but one that had occurred in practice. For example, the Sages required the dating of a *Get* (Bill of Divorce) as the result of a case in which a husband, in order to save his adulterous wife, took advantage of an undated *Get*. He gave her an undated *Get* after her act of adultery and dated it prior to the act, so that to the *Bet Din* she appeared to be an unmarried woman at the relevant time. [1]

The Rabbinic prohibition against taking a hot bath on Sabbath is another example. At one time, this was permissible, provided, of course, that the bath water had been heated before the Sabbath. The Rabbis found, however, that the bath attendants were heating water on the Sabbath and, whenever they were challenged, claiming that they had done it on the previous day. The Sages, accordingly, prohibited the taking of hot baths on Sabbath. [2]

The Sages also found that people following a number of specific occupations were particularly exposed to temptation, and they therefore stepped in to provide preventive legislation. They prohibited the purchase of wool, milk or kids from herdsmen, and the purchase of wood or fruit from those whose job was to watch over fruit trees. [3]

1   *Giṭṭin* 17A and *Jerus. Giṭṭin* IV, 3.
2   *Shabbat* 40A.
3   *Baba Kama* X, 9.

Although we have no definite evidence for this, it is probable that most *Gezerot* and *Takkanot* followed as the result of actual events which proved the need for special legislation. If we take the Sabbath laws again as an example, it is probable that the thirty-nine types of work which are prohibited by Sinaitic law in the course of time proved insufficient to achieve the ideal of a holy Sabbath day. Therefore, Rabbinic prohibitions like those directed against conducting business and handling of *Mukzeh* objects had to be enacted in order to ensure that the Sabbath day was restored to its position as a holy day, set aside for study and prayer and for family and friends. Possibly, later generations had not the same self-discipline as their ancestors had at the time of Sinai, and consequently, men who were engaged in business — which was permitted by Sinaitic law — came to write and carry and do many other things which Sinaitic law prohibited. Hence the Sages stepped in with preventive legislation creating a fence round the Torah, a fence which, in order to protect the Torah, had to become more extensive as the people became more lax in their observance.

The Four Objects of Rabbinic Enactments

While it is difficult to establish historically what motivated the Sages to enact any given decree at any particular time, the underlying purpose of *Gezerot* and *Takkanot* in general is not hard to discover. Their purpose is perhaps best summed up by Rabbi N.S. Greenspan, the late Principal of the London Yeshivah Etz Chaim, who says [4] that *Gezerot* were intended to guard against the transgression of a *Mizveh*, and *Takkanot* were intended to improve and advance one of the following :

        1. Religion

        2. The Family

4   *Melekhet Mahshebet* (London, 1955) p. 134 *et. seq.*

3. National Consciousness
4. Society

Here it should be remarked that just as the Torah never restricted its teachings and laws to matters of "religion" in the narrow sense, but was concerned with every aspect of life, so the Rabbis were concerned in the course of their legislation with every aspect of Jewish life, whether secular or religious. They legislated against dealing in weapons or animals which were unsafe, [5] just as they legislated against dealing in food which was not *kasher*. [6] They prohibited the consumption of food which had been exposed to serpents and snakes, [7] just as they prohibited food which had been cooked on Sabbath.[8] Hence, while the Sages made provisions for the advancement of religious life by instituting the reading of the Torah in public, benedictions and prayers and so on; they were equally concerned with the advancement of the family, of the nation and of society. Some examples of Rabbinic decrees intended to serve those purposes will be mentioned by way of illustration.

The *Takkanot* in the sphere of family law laid particular emphasis on the welfare of the woman. *Takkanot* were enacted to protect the interest of young girls, who were to take precedence over their brothers in matters of inheritance and who could never be altogether disinherited. [9] The position of the married woman was also secured by many *Takkanot*, [10] and the general rabbinic prin-

---

5   *Aboda Zara* I, 7.
6   *Shebiit* VII, 3.
7   *Ḥulin* II, 5. *Terumot* VIII, 4 and 5.
8   *Shabbat* 15A.
9   i.e. the daughters were entiled to maintenance out of the inheritence, *Even Haezer* 112.
10 The husband is bound to pay for her to be healed from sickness or redeemed from captivity (*Ketubot* 51A) and to arrange for her funeral (*ibid.* 46B).

ciple was that "a man was to love his wife like himself and to honour her even more." [11] Even minor details did not escape attention, for example Ezra instituted "that pedlars of cosmetics should call in all towns, so that cosmetics should be readily available and a wife should not be unattractive for her husband." [12] Further *Takkanot* protected the divorced woman and the widow. [13] On the other hand, there were *Takkanot* which regulated the duty of a woman towards her husband, [14] and finally, *Takkanot* which regulated the duty of parents to their children and vice versa. [15]

Of the enactments intended to promote national consciousness, Ḥanukkah and Purim are the best known, but there were many other special days which had been set aside to commemorate God's deliverance of his people out of the enemy's hands. On the other hand, there were days of remembrance for national catastrophes, and above all there were *Takkanot* like those of R. Johanan to commemorate the destruction of the Temple.

Enactments for the welfare of society included the various *Takkanot* instituted to regulate claims in civil law and the collection of debts, and the many *Takkanot* instituted for the sake of peace and equity. [16] The Sages were particularly concerned to establish proper standards of honesty. They extended the definition of "theft" to include gambling with dice and pigeon-racing; [17] taking an animal caught in a trap which had been set by another person; [18] attracting a swarm of bees away from their owner; [19] the gathering by one poor man of olives which had been shaken from a tree by another. [18]

---

11 *Yebamot* 62A.
12 *Baba Kama* 82A.
13 *Jerus. Ketubot* XI, 3; *Ketubot* 95B.
14 *Ketubot* 46B.
15 *Kiddushin* 29A; *Ketubot* 65B, *see also Note* 30 *p.* 81 *ante.*
16 *Gittin* 59A and B
17 *Sanhedrin* 25B.
18 *Gittin* V, 8.

Takkanot and Gezerot distinguished

In conclusion, it must be stated that while there is no cause to quarrel with Greenspan's definition of the aims of Rabbinic legislation, not all are agreed with the distinction which he draws between *Takkanot* and *Gezerot*. As has been stated according to Greenspan, the former were enacted in order to further one of the four causes which have been mentioned, whereas the latter were enacted solely to guard against the transgression of a *Mizvah*. Chajes [20] is among those who take a different view. He claims that *Gezerot* are enactments which are negative in the sense that they prohibit certain action, whereas *Takkanot* are positive in the sense that they require actions to be taken. Although the view of Chajes is generally followed, it does create difficulties. There are, in fact, a number of instances in the Talmud in which a negative prohibition is described as a *Takkanah*. For instance, the prohibition against re-marrying one's wife after having divorced her on account of her bad repute; [21] and against purchasing Jewish ritual articles from heathens, where the price charged is excessive, [22] are described as *Takkanot*, whereas according to the definition of Chajes, they should have been described as *Gezerot,* because they are negative in nature. If, on the other hand, Greenspan's definition is followed these cases present no difficulty. The prohibition against re-marrying a woman divorced on account of her bad repute is properly described as a *Takkanah,* because it tends to promote family welfare. Similarly, the prohibition against purchasing ritual articles from heathens at excessive prices is properly described as a *Takkanah,* because it tends to promote national consciousness by preventing foreign exploitation.

19   *Baba Kama* X, 2.
20   *op. cit.*
21   *Gittin* 45B.
22   *Ibid.*

SECTION III

THE OBLIGATION TO OBSERVE LAWS CREATED BY RABBINIC LEGISLATION

It has been seen [1] that the obligation to observe the laws produced by the Sages in *interpreting* the Torah is based upon the verse "If there be any matter too hard for thee in judgment... and thou shalt come unto the Priest, the Levite and the Judge that shall be in those days and enquire... and thou shalt observe to do according to all that they inform thee." [2]

Scriptural Authority for Rabbinic Legislation

It is generally accepted that *Takkanot* and *Gezerot* too have the force of law and the question will be asked "From what source do these decrees of the Sages derive their force and validity?"

The View of Maimonides

In his *Sefer Hamizvot,* [3] Maimonides states that Rabbinic decrees have the sanction of law, because the Torah declares them to be binding. The quotation from Deuteronomy cited in the previous paragraph concludes with the words "thou shalt not depart from the words that they shall tell thee" and Maimonides states

---

1   *ante* p. 58.
2   Deut. XVII, 8 and 9.
3   *Shoresh* I, See also *Mamrim* I, 2.

that this imposes a binding duty to observe all Rabbinic legislation. [4]

This view causes some difficulty. It has been seen [3] that there are a
number of differences between (*d'Oraita*) Torah legislation and
(*d'Rabanan*) Rabbinic legislation. It has been said that a person who is
in doubt whether he has already fulfilled a certain legal duty, for
example whether he has already listened to the *Shofar*, will be obliged
to listen to the *Shofar* for what may be a second time because this is a
duty imposed by the Torah. If the duty concerned is one imposed by
Rabbinic legislation, as for instance the obligation to wash one's hands
before eating bread, he will not be obliged in similar circumstances to
wash his hands for what may be a second time.

The Objection of Nachmanides

It will be objected that if the obligation to observe Torah law
and also the obligation to observe Rabbinic laws both flow from
the Torah, there should be no distinction between the two types
of law. Consequently, there would be no justification for the rule
that laws which have the status of *d'Oraita* have to be treated more
strictly and laws which have the status of *d'Rabanan* have to be
treated with greater leniency. This criticism is made by Nachmanides in his commentary on *Sefer Hamizvot*. [6]

In fact, however, as Nachmanides himself remarks, this objection may be overcome. It rests on the assumption that, because
Israel entered into a covenant at Sinai to observe all the *Mizvot* of
the Torah, all *Mizvot* of the Torah comprised in that covenant
must have equal status. The duty to observe Sabbath, the duty to

4   In this he follows a view expressed in the Talmud, *Shabbat* 23A.
5   *ante* p. 59 and Note 7.
6   *ad. loc.*

observe the dietary laws, and the duty to listen to the Sages, are of equal binding force. Either every *Mizvah* must be observed even by a person who is in doubt whether he has complied with it, or no *Mizvah* need be observed by a person in that position. This, however, is not necessarily so. The duty to listen to the Sages depends upon *what* the Sages have decreed. If, therefore, the Sages themselves decreed that a person who is in doubt whether a Rabbinic obligation applies to him (like the person who is not sure if he properly washed his hands for bread) is freed from any obligation; then, surely, the duty to listen to the Sages is limited by what the Sages have themselves decreed.

Accordingly, a person who is in doubt whether he has properly performed the *Mizvah* of *netilat yadayim* for bread is freed from the obligation to wash again, not because the duty to listen to the Sages is of a lower status than the duty to observe the Sabbath, but because the duty to listen to the Sages must be taken to its logical conclusion. If one is obliged to listen to the Sages, one is obliged — or entitled — to listen to the Sages even when they say that a person who is in doubt whether he has properly performed *netilat yadayim* need not wash again.

A View that Rabbinic Enactments may not express the Will of God

The author of *Meshekh Ḥakhmah* [7] has a completely different approach. He questions the assumption that laws with the same source of obligation must have the same degree of obligation.

He claims that there is a different degree of obligation for laws specifically given at Sinai and for laws which were authorised, but which were not specified, at Sinai. This is so, because the former laws express the Will of God, whose Will it is that the Sages shall be obeyed as much as that the Sabbath and the dietary

7 *Deut. XVII, 11.

laws shall be observed. His Will, however, is not specifically concerned that one's hands be washed before eating bread. By way of analogy, he argues that whereas God made it a *Mizvah* to obey the King and it is His Will that the King be obeyed, it cannot be said that every command of the King expresses the will of God.

This view, that only the general *Mizvah* of listening to the Sages coincides with the Will of God, but that the individual *Mizvah* ordained by the Sages, for example washing one's hands for bread, does not necessarily coincide with the Will of God, is not shared by Rabbi E. Wasserman.

A View that Rabbinic Enactments always express the Will of God

In *Kuntres Divrey Sofrim,*[8] one of Lithuania's great Talmudists of the inter-war period, Rabbi E. Wasserman, considers the view of Nachmanides that the obligation to observe Rabbinic decrees is not imposed by the Torah, and asks why, according to this view, Rabbinic laws are binding.[9] He suggests that Rabbinic laws have to be observed because they express the Will of God.[10] In this view the Will of God is not concerned merely that the Sages shall be obeyed in a general sense, but it is the Will of God that *netilat yadayim* be performed before eating bread because when the Sages decreed any specific act, they revealed that it is God's Will that this act shall be done.

8   *Branowitz, 1924.
9   The obligation cannot rest on any Sinaitic commandment or on "logic", otherwise it will be open to the very objection Nachmanides had raised against Maimonides; namely, that Rabbinic laws should be of equal status with Torah laws.
10 Great men can anticipate and reveal the Will of God. See *Shabbat* 88B.

In conclusion, Wasserman argues that the Will of God as expressed by Rabbinic legislation is of a lesser status than the Will of God which is expressed in the Scripture or in Sinaitic laws, and that it is this lower status of the *Mizvah* which accounts for the fact that a person need not observe Rabbinic legislation, when in doubt.

HEBREW SOURCES

SECTION I

ALL MAJOR *TAKKANOT* AND *GEZEROT* PRE-DATE
HILLEL AND SHAMMAI

10. I. I. Halevy, *Dorot Harishonim* I, 3. p. 223

כי אם שגם בנוגע לכל יסודי דרבנן לכל התקנות הכוללות, הנה לא לבד
שכולם כבר זמנם האחרון הוא זמן אנשי כנסת הגדולה לפני ימי שמעון הצדיק
כי אם שכבר אז גם נקבעו בכל יסודותיהם.

12. Z.H. Chajes, *Mavo Ha-Talmud* p. 298

הרבה גזירות נמצא אצלנו במשנה סתם, ולא נחלק בהם אדם מעולם, ולא
נוכל לברר מאיזה זמן באו אלינו, ומתי עמדו חכמי הדור למנין על גזירות
אלו, ובלי ספק כולם באו אלינו מן ב"ד הגדול, אשר נגזרו מהם במעמד שלם,
אחר שעמדו עליהם למנין.

20. I. I. Halevy, *Dorot Harishonim* Vol. I, 3 p. 221

כירה שהסיקוה בקש ובגבבא נותנין עליה תבשיל. בגפת ובעצים לא יתן
עד שיגרוף או עד שיתן את האפר.
בית שמאי אומרים חמין אבל לא תבשיל ובית הלל אומרים חמין ותבשיל.
בית שמאי אומרים נוטלין אבל לא מחזירין ובית הלל אומרים אף מחזירין.
(שבת ג א).

והדבר ידוע שכל איסור הטמנה אינו אלא מדרבנן ודברי בית שמאי ובית
הלל אינם הולכים בנוגע להאיסור, כי אם בנוגע להההיתר, היינו בנוגע לפרטי
דברי ההיתר האמורים במשנה. שעל זה שנאמר במשנה בהיתר התקנה

כשהתנור גרוף וקטום, על זה יאמרו ב"ה שהכונה שאז כבר מותר לגמרי בכל האופנים. וב"ש סוברים שאז הותר בדין המשנה רק חמין אבל לא תבשיל, וגם זה רק ליטול אבל לא להחזיר.

SECTION II

THE PURPOSE OF RABBINIC LEGISLATION

4.   Rabbi N. S. Greenspan, *Melekhet Maḥshebet* (London, 1955) p. 135

אם המטרה היא שלילית הרחקה מן העברה, תקון זה הוא "גזירה" ואם המטרה היא חיובית, בין שצורת התיקון היא אזהרה, בין שהיא צווי חיובי, קום ועשה, תקון זה נכנס אל סוג "התקנות". ועצם ההבחנה בין גזירה לתקנה חשוב מאד לדינא כאשר יתבאר בס"ד. התקונים החיוביים ביחס להמטרה החיובית שאליה שאפו המתקנים, שונים הם ובכללם אתה מוצא ארבעה: תקונים בחיים הדתיים, בחיים הלאומיים, בחיי המשפחה ובחיי החברה.

SECTION III

THE OBLIGATION TO OBSERVE LAWS CREATED BY RABBINIC LEGISLATION

3.   Maimonides, *Sefer Hamiẓvot, Shoresh* I

השרש הראשון שאין ראוי למנות בכלל הזה המצות שהן מדרבנן:
דע כי זה הענין לא היה ראוי לעורר עליו לבאר, כי אחר שהיה לשון התלמוד (מכות כ"ג) תרי"ג מצות נאמרו למשה בסיני איך נאמר בדבר ההוא שהוא מדרבנן שהוא מכלל המנין, אבל העירונו עליו מפני שטעו בו רבים ומנו נר חנוכה ומקרא מגילה מכלל מצות עשה .....
ומה שיראה לי שהביאם אל זה היותנו מברכין אשר קדשנו במצותיו וצונו ושאלת התלמוד (שבת כ"ג) היכן צונו ואמרו מלא תסור. ואם מטעם זה מנו

אותם הנה ראוי שימנו כל דבר שהוא מדרבנן כי כל מה שצוונו חכמים לעשותו
וכל מה שהזהירונו ממנו כבר צוה משה רבינו ע״ה בסיני שהוא צונו לעשותו
והוא אמרו ״על פי התורה אשר יורוך וגו׳״. והזהירנו יתברך מעבור דבר
מכל מה שתקנו אותו או גזרו ואמר לא תסור. וגו׳.

4. *Shabbat* 23A

אמר רב המדליק נר של חנוכה צריך לברך ... מאי מברך ? מברך אשר
קדשנו במצוותיו וצונו להדליק נר של חנוכה. והיכן צונו ? רב אויא אמר ״מלא
תסור״ (דברים י״ז). רב נחמיה אמר ״שאל אביך ויגדך זקניך ויאמרו לך״
(דברים ל״ב).

6. Nachmanides, *ad. loc.*

וכללו של דבר שדברי סופרים חלוקים הם בכל דיניהם מדברי תורה להקל
באלו ולהחמיר באלו. ואם היה העובר על דבריהם או שאינו מקיים מצות שלהם
עובר על עשה ועל לא תעשה היה חומר גדול בהם ולא היה ראויין לקולות
הללו, ... ואולי תתעקש לדעת הרב כי מה שאמרו בכל מקום להקל בדברי
סופרים הוא במחילה ובתנאי מאתם שהם התנו בגזירות ובסייגים שעשו לתורה
וכן במצות שלהם שנלך בהם לקולא כדי לחלק ולהפריש בין מה שהוא דבר
תורה ובין מה שהוא מדבריהם אע״פ שבכל אנו מצווין מן התורה. ולא היו
ספיקות שבדבריהם ראויות להתיר אותן אלא מפני התנאי הזה שעשו בהן
בתחלתן. ואין אלו דברים הגונים ולא של עיקר ...
ומ״מ כללי הרב משתבשין אבל הדבר האמיתי המנוקה מכל שבוש הוא שנודיע
שאין הלאו הזה לא תסור אלא במה שאמרו בפירוש התורה כגון הדברים הנדרשים
בגזירה שוה או בבנין אב ושאר שלש עשרה מדות שהתורה נדרשת בהן או
במשמעות לשון הכתוב עצמו וכן במה שקבלו הלכה למשה מסיני תורה שבעל
פה ...... אבל הגזירות והתקנות שעשו חכמים למשמרת התורה ולגדר שלה
אין להם בלאו הזה אלא סמך בעלמא.

7. *Meshekh Ḥokhma, Parshat Shoftim*

האמת כדברי רמב״ם, והעיקר הוא זה, כי התורה רצתה מלבד ענינים
הנצחים והקיימים לעד, יתחדש ענינים, סייגים, ואזהרות, וחומרות אשר יהיו
זמניים, היינו שיהיה ביד החכמים להוסיף עפ״י גדרים הנמסר להם, ואם יעמוד
ב״ד אחר גדול בחכמה ובמנין ובהסכם כלל ישראל, כפי הגדרים שיש בזה,
הרשות בידם לבטל, ולמען שלא ימצא איש אחד לאמור אני הרואה ואינני

כפוף לחכמי ישראל, נתנה התורה גדר לא תסור כו', שאל"כ יהיה תורה
מסורה ביד כ"א, ויעשו אגודות..... ואם כן המצוה דוקא לשמוע מה שיאמרו,
אבל העניז בעצמו מה שאמרו וחדשו, אפשר דאינו מתקבל אל רצון הבורא....
ורצה דוקא שנשמע בקולם, אבל לא בפרטי הדברים· ומצאנו דוגמתו בתורה
עניז דומה לזה, מה שהחמירה תורה לשמוע בקול מלך.... ובכל זה לדוגמא
שמעי בן גרא היה מצוה מן השם לשמוע בקול שלמה, לבלי לצאת מקיר העיר
וחוצה וחייב מיתה ע"ז, אבל האם רצה השם שיאמר זה שלמה?.....

ככה שמה התורה לחוק לבנ"י לשמוע בקול חז"ל כקול מלך, מאז מלכי רבנז.
אבל בפרטי העניז אין רצונו בצווי פרטי.

ומעתה נבאר כל השגותיו, כי מספקא לן בדברי תורה, שמא הוא חזיר...
א"כ אכלנו חזיר דבר המתועב באמת, אבל בספק עירוב, א"כ כיון שהעניז
הזה אינו בפרט רצון הבורא, רק שצוה לשמוע אליהם, וכיון שע"ז לא דברו,
א"כ לא נקרא מי שאינו עושה כן, שאינו שומע בקולם.

8.   *Kuntres Divrey Sofrim* (Branovitz, 1924) p. 6

נראה מדברי הרמב"ן, ממה שהוכיח מדמצינו שדבריהם קלין יותר מדאורייתא
שלדבריו אין בדבריהם שום דאורייתא כלל. דאם נאמר שהרמב"ן לא חלק על
הרמב"ם רק לעניז קרא דלא תסור, אבל גם הוא מודה שנצטוינו מן התורה
לשמוע לדברי חכמים מקרא או מסברא או מהלכה למשה מסיני. אם כן הקושיות
שהקשה על הרמב"ם מפני מה דבריהם קלין משל תורה, נאמר לו ולטעמיה
גם כן יקשה זאת הקושיא בעצמה. ומה נפקא מיניה, בזה אם נצטוינו לשמוע
לדברי חכמים מקרא "דלא תסור" או מקרא אחרינא או מהלכה למשה מסיני
..... אלא ע"כ צ"ל לכאורה לדעת הרמב"ן שלא נצטוינו כלל מן התורה לשמוע
לדברי חכמים.

ותימה גדולה לומר כן, דאם כן מאיזה טעם אנו חייבין לשמוע להן?.....
יש לומר..... בכל המצוות והאיסורין של דבריהן הסכימה דעתן לדעת
המקום..... ומהאי טעמא אנו חייבין לעשות כדבריהם, שהרי אנו מקיימין
בזה רצון השי"ת שהסכימה דעתן לדעתו, ומכל מקום, כיון שלא בא ציווי
מפורש בתורה הן קלין מדברי תורה המפורשין.

RESTRICTIONS ON RABBINIC LEGISLATION

RESTRICTIONS ON RABBINIC LEGISLATION

INTRODUCTION

In the unequal partnership between Sinaitic and Rabbinic law, the former played the dominant part and imposed limitations on the latter. Sinaitic Law restricted the manner in which the Sages were entitled to present their legislation and in general circumscribed the legislative powers of the Sages. These limitations are important in that they helped to preserve the Divine element in the Oral Law; and they will be considered in three sections which will show that:

1. Rabbinic legislation was not to be misrepresented as though it were inspired by prophecy.
2. Nor was it to be misrepresented as though it were Torah legislation.
3. Torah law and decisions of an earlier *Bet Din*, as well as the will of the people, imposed certain restrictions on the legislative powers of the Sages.

SECTION I

PROPHECY AND LEGISLATION

The Sages could not claim prophetic revelation as the source of their legislation, because once the Torah had been given at Sinai, prophetic revelation ceased to be relevant. The Torah had been given

and it was unalterable. Even God himself would not alter it. [1]
What then could prophecy add to the Oral Law? Revelation was
completed and now only interpretation could follow.

Maimonides states the rule as follows: — Because "the Torah is
not in heaven," [2] a prophet cannot claim competence to produce new
laws. Furthermore, even if the prophet states the law in accordance
with *Halachah*, the fact that he claims prophetic inspiration as the
source of his statement renders him a false prophet. [3]

Did the prophets, in fact, try to influence and change *Halachah*? To what extent do the early sources support the rules propounded by Maimonides?

In the Talmud, we find conflicting authorities on the point.
On the one hand the intervention in a matter of *Halachah* by a
heavenly voice — *Bat Kol* — was completely rejected by R.
Joshua. [4] It is also reported that both Joshua, and later, Samuel
refused to enquire in heaven regarding forgotten *Halachot*, because "no prophet may produce any new laws." [5] On the other
hand, it is reported in *Massekhet Megillah* that the prophets re-
established certain laws which had been forgotten." [6]

However, the rule as propounded by Maimonides is not, in
fact, contradicted by the case in *Massekhet Megillah*. A distinction
must be drawn between the prophet acting in his capacity as a Sage
and spiritual leader and the prophet acting as a man with a message

---

1 Maimonides: the ninth of the Thirteen Principles of Faith as interpreted
   in *Ani Maamin* Prayer.
2 *Baba Meẓia* 59B.
3 Maimonides *Yesodey Hatorah* IX, 4 and see Kesef Mishneh, *ad. loc.*
4 *Baba Meẓia* 59B, but see Tosefot *ad. loc.* that occasionally the decision
   of *Bat Kol* is accepted, e.g. in the dispute between Bet Shammai and
   Bet Hillel. See infra p. 154. See also *Iggeret Moshe* (R. Moshe Feinstein) *Oraḥ Ḥayyim* Responsum No. 14.
5 *Temurah* 16A.
6 *Megillah* 2B and 3A.

from God. [7] In the first capacity the prophet is under no disability; there is accordingly, no objection to a prophet re-establishing forgotten laws, provided he does not act as a prophet, but relies on his wisdom and knowledge of the Torah.

Hora'at Sha'ah

Similarly, in his capacity as the spiritual leader of the people, the prophet was entitled to invoke the power of *Hora'at Sha'ah*. This power entitles the prophet or the *Bet Dīn Hagadol*, exceptionally, to suspend the application of Torah law, provided: [8]

1. The suspension of the Torah law is not on a permanent basis.
2. The purpose of such suspension is to strengthen Torah law generally. [9]

The classical case of a prophet exercising the power of

---

7 This distinction is drawn by Z.H. Chajes, *Torat Haneviim, Ele Hamiẓvot*, Chapter I.

8 Whether (1) and (2) are alternatives or cumulatives is not clear. Maimonides stresses the temporary basis of *Hora'at Sha'ah* (*Yesodey Hatorah* IX, 3). Rashi and Meiri, *Yebamot* (90B) stress only (2). The difference of opinion may turn on the interpretation of the expression "*Lefi Sha'ah*" (*Yebamot, loc. cit.*). Does it mean temporary, or according to the requirement of the time, or both?

9 There is a further proviso that there is no power to permit idol worship, even as *Hora'at Sha'ah* (Maimonides, *loc. cit.*). According to the Talmud (*Yebamot, loc. cit.*) and *Sifrey*, (Deuteronomy, Section 68) the doctrine of *Hora'at Sha'ah* is based on the words (Deut. XVIII, 16) "Ye shall listen to him (the prophet)." Also Psalm 119 Verse 126 is interpreted as giving authority to "destroy of his law because it is a time to act for God." See *Temurah* 14B, *Berakhot* 54A and 63A, *Yoma* 69A and Rashi, *ad. loc.* and Kimchi commentary on Psalms.

Hora'at Sha'ah is that of Elijah on Mount Carmel, [10] when, contrary to Torah law, he brought burnt offerings outside the precincts of the Temple. But there were other such incidents, [11] like the offerings by Joshua at Mount Ebal, [12] or by Gideon at the stronghold, [13] or by Manoah on the rock. [14] In all these cases, it appears that the Torah law which required sacrifices to be brought exclusively within the precincts of the Temple [15] was transgressed. There are even instances of the death sentence being executed contrary

10 "And Ahab sent unto all the children of Israel, and gathered the prophets together unto Mount Carmel. And Elijah came near unto all the people, and said: 'How long halt ye between two opinions, it the Lord be God, follow Him; but if Baal, follow him.' And the people answered him not a word, Then said Elijah unto the people: 'I, even I only, am left a prohpet of the Lord; but Baal's prophets are four hundred and fifteen men. Let them therefore give us two bullocks; and let them choose one bullock for themselves, and cut it in pieces, and lay it on the wood, and put no fire under; and I will dress the other bullock, and lay it on the wood, and put no fire under. And call ye on the name of your god, and I will call on the name of the Lord; and the God that answereth by fire, let him be God." (Kings I, XVIII, 20-24).

11 See Chajes, *op. cit.*

12 "Then Joshua built an altar unto the Lord, the God of Israel, in Mount Ebal . . . and they offered thereon burnt offerings unto the Lord, and sacrificed peace offerings," Joshua VIII, 30 and 31. See Numbers R. XIV, 1.

13 "And it came to pass on the same night, that the Lord said unto him: 'Take thy father's bullock, and the second bullock of seven years old, and throw down the altar of Baal that thy fathers hath, and cut down the Asherah that is by it; and build an altar unto the Lord thy God upon the top of this stronghold, in the ordered place, and take the second bullock, and offer a burnt offering with the wood of the Asherah which thou shalt cut down'" (Judges VI, 25-27). See *Temurah* 28B.

14 "So Manoah took the kids with the meal-offering, and offered it upon the rock unto the Lord" (Judges XIII, 19). See *Zebahim* 119B.

15 Deut. XII, 13.

to established principles. The *Megadef* [16] was sentenced to death, although at the time of his offence the penalty had not been fixed. Achan [17] and the Amalekite [18] were both executed, although it was their own confession which had convicted them. If the normal Torah laws had been applied in any of these cases, the death penalty could never have been inflicted.

Although in some of these cases, there was an express command of God which required the prophet to act otherwise than in accordance with established law, the Tosafists [19] state [20] that such express authority from God is not essential for *Hora'at Sha'ah* to operate.

In these cases the prophet does not in fact act as a prophet,

---

16 "And the Israelitish woman's son uttered blasphemously the name and execrated... And they placed him in ward, that the mind of the Eternal might be showed them. And the Eternal spake unto Moses saying '.... Let all the congregation of Israel overwhelm him with stones'" (Leviticus XXIV, 11-14). See *Ramah* Sanhedrin 78B and *Divrey David*, Lev. XXIV, 12.

17 "And Joshua said unto Achan: 'My son, give, I pray thee, glory to the Lord, the God of Israel, and make confession unto Him; and tell me now what thou hast done; hide nothing from me.' And Achan answered Joshua and said: 'Of a truth I have sinned against the Lord, the God of Israel, and thus and thus have I done.'" (Joshua VII, 19-25). See Maimonides, *loc. cit.* Abarbanel and Ralbag.

18 "And David said unto the young man that told him: 'How knowest thou that Saul and Jonathan his son are dead?'... And he said unto me: Stand, I pray thee, beside me, and slay me, for the agony hath taken hold of me; because my life is just yet in me. So I stood beside him, and slew him" (2 Samuel I, 5-15).

19 Tosafists were the authors of Tosefot, explanatory glosses on the Talmud. They were mostly of French and German origin and date from the twelfth and thirteenth centuries.

20 *Tosefot Yeshanim, Yebamot* 90B *"Kemo"; *Tosefot, ad. loc. "Veligmor";* Sanhedrin 89B *"Elija";* Meiri, *ad. loc.; Minḥat Ḥinnukh,* Miẓvah 516; but according to *Minḥat Ḥinnukh,* Maimonides does not share this view.

but with the same authority with which the *Bet Din Hagadol* [21] was invested. The Talmud [22] reports a case in which the *Bet Din Hagadol* invoked its power of *Hora'at Sha'ah*. This was during the Greek occupation of the Holy Land, when a man rode on a horse on the Sabbath. The *Bet Din* ordered him to be stoned. "This was done not because it was the proper punishment, but because the particular time required such action."

The Prophets and Temple Sacrifices

In dealing with Prophecy and legislation, it is necessary to mention the often repeated allegation that the Prophets aspired to change the Pentateuchal Laws concerning Temple sacrifices.

The problem of the prophets and their attitude to Temple sacrifices, it has been pointed out, resolves itself upon a thorough examination of the relevant texts in the books of Samuel, [23] Isaiah, [24] and the latter prophets. [25] It will become quite clear that

---

21 Maimonides, *Sanhedrin* XXIV, 4 and *Mamrim* II, 4. This power is limited to *Bet Din Hagadol* according to Ra'avad, *Mamrim* II, 9; *Ḥiddushey Ran, Sanhedrin* 46A; *Nemukey Yosef, Sanhedrin* 52B; but it is not limited according to Meiri, *Sanhedrin* 52; Rashba, *Responsa* V, 238 and *Tor Ḥoshen Mishpat*.

22 *Yebamot 90B.

23 "Hath the Lord as great delight in burnt offerings and sacrifices as in the hearkening to the voice of the Lord? Behold to obey is better than sacrifices and to hearken than the fat of rams," (I Samuel, XV, 22).

24 "To what purpose is the multitude of your sacrifices unto Me? Saith the Lord ... I cannot endure iniquity along with the solemn assembly ... Yea, when ye make many prayers I will not hear, your hands are full of blood" (Isaiah I, 11-27).

25 "For I desire mercy not sacrifices" (Hosea VI, 6). "Neither will I regard the peace offerings of your fat beasts. Take thou away from Me the noise of thy songs and let me not hear the melody of thy Psalteries, but let justice well up as waters and righteousness as a mighty stream" (Amos V, 21-24). "Will the Lord be pleased with thousands of rams?" (Micah VI, 7).

these prophets did not object to the bringing of sacrifices, or to prayer, except by persons whose "hands are full of blood." [26] As Jeremiah [27] said, "Will ye still murder, commit adultery and offer unto Baal and walk after other gods whom ye have not known and come and stand before Me in this house?" The prophets exclaim against persons who have sunk to the depths of moral wickedness and yet turn to God in prayer and Temple sacrifice.

In no case does the Prophet protest against the observance, by morally degraded people, of *Mizvot* other than prayer and sacrifice. [28] It has not been said by any of the Prophets that God rejects the observance of *Mizvot* like Sabbath or Passover by even the most wicked individuals.

A new suggestion

We would suggest that the act of prayer and the bringing of sacrifices are different from any other *Mizvot*. They are intended to demonstrate something in relation to the person who observes these *Mizvot* — that he subjects himself to the rule of God. [29] As far as the reasons for other *Mizvot* are known, this is not so. *Mizvot* like Sabbath and Passover demonstrate something about the creation of the world and about the Exodus from Egypt. They demonstrate facts outside the person who observes them.

For a thief or a murderer to pray or to bring sacrifices is therefore to demonstrate something which is a lie. A thief or

26 Isaiah, *loc. cit.*
27 (Jeremiah VII, 2).
28 The reference to New Moon and Sabbath (Isaiah I, 13) is to sacrifices brought on those occasions. (*Mezudat David, ad. loc.*).
29 "Which is the worship of the heart? — it is prayer"(*Ta'anit* 2A).

murderer who observes Sabbath or Passover, on the other hand, still demonstrates something which is completely true.

The burden of the message of the prophets, accordingly, was not to change the mode of worship, but to change the mode of life of the worshippers.

SECTION II

THE PROHIBITION AGAINST ADDING [1] TO THE TORAH

Deuteronomy IV, 2, reads: "Ye shall not add unto the word which I command you nor shall you diminish ought from it."

This presents a problem. Does this not mean that all Rabbinic legislation is *ultra vires*? Yet the Talmud states that according to the Scripture there is the positive obligation upon the Sages to protect God's commandments by means of legislation. [2]

However, a distinction must be drawn between adding to God's Laws and creating a new system of Rabbinic Laws. By way of analogy it may be said that one does not add to the Empire State Building by erecting another building one hundred and two stories high, but by increasing the height of the existing building. Similarly, the Sages are not adding to God's laws by creating a body of Rabbinic legislation as they would be if they extended the laws of the Torah, for example, by adding an eighth day to *Sukkot* or by putting five fringes on the *Tallit*.

---

1 The discussion which follows centres round the prohibition against *adding* to the commandment of the Torah *mutatis mutandis*, the same principles apply to the prohibition against *detracting* therefrom.

2 *Yebamot* 21A.

Two ways of adding to the Torah

(a)

The prohibition against adding to the Torah would be relevant however had the Sages wanted to present their laws as if they were the Laws of the Torah, to revert to our analogy, one may add to the number of Empire State Buildings, if one erects another building of one hundred and two stories and calls the newly erected building by the same name. So, also one may be adding to God's laws if one puts forward Rabbinic legislation, as if it were God's command. Accordingly, Nachmanides [3] declares that the prohibition against adding to God's laws is not infringed, provided that "it is made clear that the particular laws have been made as a fence round the Torah and are not from the Torah." Likewise, Maimonides [4] writes that the prohibition is not violated if the Rabbis declare unequivocally that what they ordain is of Rabbinic origin and do not treat their own laws as if they were Torah laws.

This then presents a restriction upon the manner in which the Sages could legislate, namely, that they could not claim the authority of the Torah laws for their own legislation.

(b)

The prohibition "thou shalt not add thereto (to the Law of the Torah) nor diminish from it" would be relevant had the Sages wanted to extend the Laws of the Torah by requiring the performing of a *Mizvah* at a time when, according to the Torah, it does not apply. For example, it prohibits the sitting in the *Sukkah* for eight days when the Torah had prescribed that one

---

3 *Deut.* IV, 2.
4 *Mamrim* II, 9. Ravad, *ad. loc.* disagrees and see also *Or Sameah, ad. loc.* See also *Sefer Hahinnukh, Mizvah* 454.
5 *Rosh Hashanah* 28B.

should do so for seven days only.[5] It also prohibits the performing of a *Mizvah* with additional objects. For example, it prohibits the fixing of a fifth fringe to a *Tallit* when the Torah had prescribed only four.[6]

According to Rashba[7] these further restrictions did not apply to Rabbinic *Takkanot* and *Gezerot*, because they were enacted to protect Torah law.[8] So that, for example, the *Takkanah* of a second day *Yom Tov*,[9] was perfectly legitimate.

Other commentators[10] claim that in any event the second day *Yom-Tov* does not constitute a contravention of the prohibition against adding to the laws of the Torah. They explain that the second day was not intended to add to the *Yom Tov* ordained by the Torah, but to make sure that the correct day was kept, and therefore both days were, in fact, observed with the intention of keeping the proper first day.

6   *Sifrey*, Deut. XIII, 1 Sec, 55. *Sanhedrin* 88B. Yosef Albo, *op. cit.* III, 14 states "The Torah does not warn against adding to the number of *Mizvot*, but against adding something to the method of performing the *Mizvot*."

7   Solomon b. Abraham Aderet, 13th Century Spanish Talmudist.

8   *Rosh Hashanah* 16B.

9   It should be explained that a new month would be declared either after 29 or after 30 days, in either case counting from the 1st day of the previous month. If the Sanhedrin in Jerusalem had received evidence on the 30th day that the New Moon had been seen, that day would be declared as the 1st of the next month, otherwise the following day would be so declared. Until they had received news from Jerusalem, a distant settlement did not know which of two days was the first of the month. Accordingly, in order to make sure of observing the correct day *Yom Tov*, they had to keep *Yom Tov* on two days. This applied even to a *Yom Tov*, which came only on the 15th of the month, because the news frequently took longer than 15 days to reach outlying parts.

10 See Rashi, *Erubin* 96A and *Shiltey Hagiborim, Rosh Hashanah* IV.

SECTION III

THE WILL OF GOD, THE WILL OF *BET DIN*
AND THE WILL OF THE PEOPLE

The Sages were further restricted in their legislative powers by:
    I. the Will of God
    II. the will of *Bet Din*
    III. the will of the people.

I

The Will of God as expressed by Sinaitic laws was absolutely binding on the Sages. "Have then the Sages power to uproot this law of the Torah?" the Sages asked. [1]

Yet, in exceptional circumstances, the Torah empowered the Sages to legislate contrary to Sinaitic law. Exactly what these circumstances were is a matter of dispute between the great, early scholars. [2] One rule, however, is clearly stated in the Talmud, [3] namely, that the Sages were entitled to decree that an action which the Torah required to be done, should *not* be done. They could prevent a person from carrying out an act required by the Torah, as distinct from requiring him to carry out an act prohibited by the Torah. The distinction which is made is one between an act of commission and an act of omission.

The Rabbinic prohibition against blowing the *Shofar* when *Rosh Hashanah* coincides with the Sabbath is a case in point. The Torah had ordained that the *Shofar* must be blown on *Rosh Hashanah*, and the Torah had made no distinction between *Rosh Hashanah*, during mid-week and *Rosh Hashanah* when it coincides

---

1 *See* *Giṭṭin* 36A.
2 *Yebamot* 88A, *Tosefot* "*Mitoch*" and *Nemukey Yosef, ad. loc.*
3 *Giṭṭin* 36B.

with Sabbath. The Sages, however, were afraid that the *Shofar* might come to be carried through the streets on Sabbath, so they decreed that this law requiring the *Shofar* to be blown on *Rosh Hashanah* shall not apply when *Rosh Hashanah* coincides with Sabbath.[3a]

As in the case of *Shofar,* so also in all other cases [4] where the Sages decided to legislate against Torah law in the manner described, they did so in order to protect some other law against transgression. They thought it better that a law of the Torah should be allowed to go by default than that another law should be actively transgressed. They preferred that the *Mizvah* of *Shofar* should go by default when *Rosh Hashanah* coincides with Sabbath, rather than that, forgetting the prohibition against carrying on Sabbath, someone should carry the *Shofar* through the streets and a prohibition against carrying on the Sabbath be actively transgressed.

II

Not only a *Halachah* from Sinai, but also a *Halachah* of an earlier *Bet Din* was binding on the Sages. When a *Bet Din* had decided a question of *Halachah* this decision became part of the body of the Oral Law and no later *Bet Din* could reverse this decision "unless it was greater in wisdom and numbers." [5]

3a **Rosh Hashanah* 29B.

4 See the six classical cases cited *Yebamot* 90B and see *Pesahim* VI, 1; and VIII, 8; *Sabbath* 130B and *Menahot* and see Chajes, *Darkey Hahorah* II.

5 **Eduyot* I, 5; Maimonides, *Mamrim* II, 2. Because the *Bet Din Hagadol* never varied from the prescribed number of 71 members, "greater in numbers" cannot have its natural meaning and has been variously interpreted to mean that it has more sages following its decisions (Maimonides, *loc. cit.*) or more pupils at its *Yeshivah* (Bartenura, *Eduyot, ad. loc.*) or even that it is presided over by an older *Ab Bet Din* (*Tiferet Yisrael* and *Tosefot Yom Tov, ad. loc.*).

Even a change of circumstances would not automatically annul the decision of an earlier *Bet Din*.[6] For example, the *Mishnah* reports a Rabbinic decree prohibiting the redemption of the fruit of any four-year-old vineyard (*Neta Revai*) near Jerusalem. It had to be taken to Jerusalem and eaten there "so that the streets of Jerusalem should be decked with fruit"; and this decree continued in force, even after the destruction of the Temple, and even though there was no purpose in having the streets of conquered Jerusalem decked with fruit. Only when R. Johanan and his *Bet Din* eventually abolished this decree was it again possible to redeem the fruit and take the money to Jerusalem instead. [7]

Where the Sages, in making a decree, had intended that it should cease to apply in changed circumstances; new circumstances render, the decree obsolete, without any further action on the part of a *Bet Din*. [8] The Tosefists [9] claim that Rabbinic decrees like that against drinking uncovered water or that against trading with non-Jews on their holy days automatically ceased to apply when circumstances changed. This is so, because the law against drinking uncovered water had been enacted in a time and in countries where snakes were prevalent, and the law against trading with non-Jews on their holy days had been enacted in times of idol-worship, when non-Jews were wont to bless their idols for their good fortune. The Tosefists assume that when these laws were enacted, they were never intended for different circumstances in other countries. These decrees, therefore, became obsolete, and the authority of a *Bet Din* was not required to abolish them.

---

6 See *Beẓah* 5A, see Ra'avad and Radbaz comments on Maimonides *loc. cit.*; *Aboda Zara* 36A; Rosh, *Responsa* II, 8; *Ḥiddushey Ran, Sanhedrin* 59B.

7 *Beẓah* 5B.

8 *Ḥiddushey Meiri, Aboda Zara* 36A; *Pri Ḥadash, Yoreh Deah* 116.

9 *Tosefot, Aboda Zara* 35A "*Ḥodo*". *Ibid.* 57B "*Afukey*", but see *Pesaḥim*, 50A "*Makom*".

III

Finally, the will of the people restricted the legislative power of the Sages. Maimonides expresses the rule thus: "Before instituting a decree or enacting an ordinance or introducing a custom which it is deemed necessary, *Bet Din* must calmly deliberate and make sure that the majority of the community can live up to it. At no time is a decree to be imposed upon the public, which the majority thereof cannot endure." [10] It is in this sense that the expression "will of the people" is used here. For example, the Sages were concerned that animals strayed into other people's fields and ate the crops. They, accordingly, decided to restrict the rearing of animals. However, out of consideration for the convenience of the people, they limited their restriction to sheep, which could be imported from other countries and excluded cattle, which could not. [11] Again in order to avoid hardship, they refused to prohibit produce of a field which had been ploughed during the Sabbatical year, because the majority of the people would be too severely affected by such a prohibition.[12] Again, the Sages refused to decree excessive mourning for the destruction of the Temple, because it was something which the majority of the people were unable to bear. [13]

In addition to the fact that the Sages could not enact laws which the people were unable to endure, if a law had not spread widely among the people, [14] it could be abolished by a subsequent

---

10   *Mamrim* II, 5.
11   **Baba Kama* 79B.
12   *Jerus. Sheviit* IV, 2; *Tosefta Sheviit* III.
13   **Baba Batra* 60B.
14   **Aboda Zara* 36A. For whether "a *Gezerah* which had not spread widely among the people" is a concept distinct from "a *Gezerah* which most people could not carry out" see Maimonides, *Mamrim* II, 3 and *Leḥem Mishneh, ad. loc.* Also Ran and Meiri, *Aboda Zara* 36A.

Bet Din, even if that *Bet Din* was neither greater in numbers nor in wisdom. [15]

These three factors, the Will of God, the will of *Bet Din* and the will of the people, circumscribed the legislative powers of the Sages. However, before it can be said with finality that the Sages were strictly confined in their development of the Oral Law within this framework, one well-recognised legal device for affecting changes in the law other than by legislation, has to be considered, and we shall turn our attention to this in the following chapter.

15 There were, in fact: 1. Decrees which only a greater *Bet Din* could abolish. 2. Decrees which even a greater *Bet Din* could not abolish. 3. Decrees which even a lesser *Bet Din* could abolish. According to some views the 18 *Gezerot* of Bet Shammai and Bet Hillel belonged to Group 2, (*Jerus. Shabbat* I, 4), at least those of the 18 *Gezerot* which had spread widely among the people. Those which had not so spread belonging to Group 3. According to other views, all decrees which had spread widely among the people belonged to Group 2.

HEBREW SOURCES

SECTION I

THE TORAH IS NOT IN HEAVEN

3. Maimonides, *Yesode Hatorah* IX, 4

וכן (נביא) אם עקר דבר מדברים שלמדנו מפי השמועה או שאמר בדין
מדיני תורה שה׳ צוה לו שהדין כך הוא והלכה כדברי פלוני הרי זה נביא
השקר ויחנק אע״פ שעשה אות שהרי בא להכחיש התורה שאמרה לא בשמים
היא. אבל לפי שעה שומעין לו בכל.

4. *Baba Meẓia* 59B

מאי עכנאי אמר ר״י אמר שמואל שהקיפו דברים כעכנא זו וטמאוהו. תנא
באותו היום השיב רבי אליעזר כל תשובות שבעולם ולא קבלו הימנו אמר
להם אם הלכה כמותי חרוב זה יוכיח נעקר חרוב ממקומו מאה אמה ואמרי לה
ארבע מאות אמה. אמרו לו אין מביאין ראיה מן החרוב. חזר ואמר להם אם הלכה
כמותי אמת המים יוכיחו. חזרו אמת המים לאחוריהם. אמרו לו אין מביאין
ראיה מאמת המים. חזר ואמר להם אם הלכה כמותי כותלי בית המדרש יוכיחו
הטו כותלי בית המדרש ליפול, גער בהם ר׳ יהושע..... יצאתה בת־קול
ואמרה מה לכם אצל ר״א שהלכה כמותו בכ״מ עמד ר״י על רגליו ואמר לא
בשמים היא. מאי לא בשמים היא ? אמר רבי ירמיה שכבר נתנה תורה מהר
סיני. אין אנו משגיחין בבת קול שכבר כתבת בהר סיני בתורה ״אחרי רבים
להטות״... אותו היום הביאו כל טהרות שטיהר ר״א ושרפום באש ונמנו
עליו וברכוהו.

5. *Temurah* 16A

אף חטאת שמתו בעליה נשתכחה בימי אבלו של משה אמרו לפנחס שאל !

אמר להם לא בשמים היא א״ל לאלעזר שאל ! אמר להם אלה המצות שאין נביא
רשאי לחדש דבר מעתה.

6. *Megillah* 2B

מנצפ״ך צופים (נביאי הדורות — רש״י) אמרום. ותסברא והכתיב ״אלה
המצוות״ (ויקרא כ״ז) שאין נביא רשאי לחדש דבר מעתה ? . . . . . אלא שכחום
וחזרו ויסדום.

HORAAT SHAAH

8. *Yebamot* 90B

ת״ש ״אליו תשמעון״ (דברים י״ח) אפילו אומר לך עבור על אחת מכל
מצוות שבתורה כגון אליהו בהר הכרמל הכל לפי שעה שמע לו ? שאני התם
דכתיב ״אליו תשמעון״. וליגמר מיניה ? מיגדר מילתא שאני :

20. *Tosefot ad. loc. "Veligmor"*

וא״ת שאני התם דעל פי הדבור היה מתנבא לעבור והיכי נגמר מיניה
לעבור משום תקנתא דרבנן שלא על פי הדיבור ? ונראה דכיון דעל פי הדבור
שרי משום צורך שעה, הוא הדין שלא על פי הדבור, שהרי אין נביא רשאי
לחדש דבר מעתה.

22. *Yebamot* 90B

א״ר אלעזר בן יעקב שמעתי שב״ד מכין ועונשין שלא מן התורה, ולא
לעבור על דברי תורה אלא לעשות סייג לתורה. ומעשה באדם אחד שרכב
על סוס בשבת בימי יונים, והביאוהו לב״ד וסקלוהו, לא מפני שראוי לכך
אלא שהשעה צריכה לכך.

SECTION II

RABBINIC LAWS MUST NOT BE PRESENTED AS TORAH LAWS

3. Nahmanides, Deut. IV, 2

ומה שתקנו חכמים משום גדר כגון שניות לעריות וכיוצא בהן כי היא מצוה
מן התורה ובלבד שידע שהם משום הגדר הזה ואינן מפי הקב״ה בתורה.

4.   *Maimonides, Mamrim* II, 9

הואיל ויש לבית דין לגזור ולאסור דבר המותר ויעמוד איסורו לדורות
וכן יש להן להתיר איסורי תורה לפי שעה מהו זה שהזהירה תורה "לא תוסיף
עליו ולא תגרע ממנו" ? שלא להוסיף על דברי תורה ולא לגרוע מהן ולקבוע
הדבר לעולם בדבר שהוא מן התורה בין בתורה שבכתב בין בתורה שבע"פ
כיצד הרי כתוב בתורה "לא תבשל גדי בחלב אמו". מפי השמועה למדו שזה
הכתוב אסר לבשל ולאכול בשר בחלב בין בשר בהמה בין בשר חיה אבל
בשר העוף מותר בחלב מן התורה, אם יבוא בית־דין ויתיר בשר חיה בחלב
הרי זה גורע. ואם יאסור בשר העוף ויאמר שהוא בכלל הגדי והוא אסור מן
התורה הרי זה מוסיף. אבל אם אמר בשר העוף מותר מן התורה ואנו נאסור
אותו ונודיע לעם שהוא גזרה ... אין זה מוסיף.

THE PROHIBITION AGAINST ADDING TO TORAH LAW
DID NOT APPLY TO *TAKKANOT* AND *GEZEROT*

8.   Rashba, *Rosh Hashanah* 16B

הקשו בתוספות "והא קא עבר משום בל תוסיף ?"

ומסתברא דלא קשי' כלל דלא אמרו התם דאיכא משום בל תוסיף אלא
במה שהוא מוסיף מדעת עצמו כגון כהן שהוסיף ברכה משלו וא"נ ישן בשמיני
בסוכה במתכוון למצוה וכיוצא באלו אבל במה שעמדו חכמים ותקנו לצורך
אין כאן בל תוסיף דכבר נאמר על פי התורה אשר יורוך.

SECTION III

RABBINICAL LAW MUST NOT CONTRAVENE TORAH LAW

1.   *Gittin* 36A

ומי איכא מידי דמדאורייתא משמטא שביעית והתקין הלל דלא משמטא ?

THE SAGES COULD DECREE THE OMISSION OF AN ACT
REQUIRED BY TORAH LAW

3.   *Gittin* 36B

ומי איכא מידי דמדאורייתא לא משמטא שביעית ותקינו רבנן דתשמט —
אמר אביי שב ואל תעשה הוא.

3a.   *Rosh Hashanah* 29B

מתני׳: יום טוב של ר״ה שחל להיות בשבת, במקדש היו תוקעין אבל לא
במדינה״. ...

גמ׳: מנה״מ... הכל חייבין בתקיעת שופר ואין הכל בקיאין בתקיעת שופר,
גזירה שמא יטלנו בידו וילך אצל הבקי ללמוד, ויעבירנו ד׳ אמות ברשות
הרבים והיינו טעמא דלולב והיינו טעמא דמגילה.

THE BINDING FORCE OF A BET DIN DECISION

5.   *Eduyyot* I, 5

שאין בית דין יכול לבטל דברי ב״ד חבירו עד שיהיה גדול ממנו בחכמה
ובמנין.

DECREES WHICH WERE NOT INTENDED TO APPLY IN
CHANGED CIRCUMSTANCES

9.   *Tosefot, Aboda Zara* 35A "Ḥodo"

ואנו שאין נחשים מצוין בינינו אין לחוש משום גלוי. ואין לומר דדבר שבמנין
הוא וצריך מנין אחר להתירו, כי ודאי הוא כשאסרו תחלה לא אסרו אלא
במקום שהנחשים מצוין.

9.   *Tosefot, Aboda Zara* 57B "Afukey"

ואע״ג דגם משא ומתן ביום אידם היה דבר שבמנין ולא הוצרך מנין אחר
להתירו להנהו דלא אזלו ומודו כי ודאי מתחילה לא גזרו עליהם.

9.   *Tosefot, Pesaḥim* 50A "Makom"

מקום שנהגו לעשות מלאכה בערבי פסחים עד חצות עושין:... מאי שנא
ערבי פסחים משאר י״ט? משום דזמן הפסח מחצות ואילך ...
ונראה דאף בזמן הזה דליכא הקרבה כיון שנאסר אז אסור לעולם.

THE WILL OF THE PEOPLE

11.   *Baba Kama* 79B

אף על פי שאמרו אין מגדלין בהמה דקה, אבל מגדלין בהמה גסה, לפי

שאין גוזרין גזרה על הצבור אלא אם רוב צבור יכולין לעמוד בה. בהמה דקה
אפשר להביא מחוץ לארץ בהמה גסה אי אפשר וכו׳.

13. *Baba Batra* 60B

כשחרב הבית בשניה רבו פרושין בישראל שלא לאכול בשר ושלא לשתות
יין. נטפל להן ר׳ יהושע אמר להן..... בני בואו ואומר לכם, שלא להתאבל
כל עיקר אי אפשר שכבר נגזרה גזרה. ולהתאבל יותר מדאי אי אפשר שאין
גוזרין גזירה על הצבור אא״כ רוב הצבור יכולין לעמוד בה.....

14. *Aboda Zara* 36A

שמן, ר׳ יהודה ובית דינו נמנו עליו והתירוהו... ור׳ יהודה הנשיא היכי
מצי למישרא תקנתא דתלמידי שמאי והלל, והתנן אין בית דין יכול לבטל דברי
בית דין חבירו אלא אם כן גדול הימנו בחכמה ובמנין. ועוד הא אמר רבה
בר בר חנה אמר ר׳ יוחנן בכל יכול לבטל בית דין דברי בית דין חברו חוץ
משמונה עשר דבר... אמר רב משרשיא מה טעם? הואיל ופשט איסורו
ברוב ישראל, שמן לא פשט איסורו ברוב ישראל... וסמכו רבותינו (רבי יהודה
הנשיא — רש״י) על... שהיו אומרים אין גוזרין גזרה על הצבור אא״כ רוב
צבור יכולין לעמוד בה.

CHAPTER V

LEGAL FICTIONS

CHAPTER V

LEGAL FICTIONS

INTRODUCTION

It has been seen that there were severe restrictions on the legislative power of the Sages. In most legal systems comparable restrictions have produced the urge to find loopholes and to create devices which circumvent unwelcome limitations. When a change in
the law was unattainable in the usual manner resort was had to
legal fictions, in order to produce by other means what could not
be achieved by legislation. In this chapter, we shall investigate
whether — in view of the limitations upon their power to legislate
— the Sages in Jewish Law made use of similar devices.

First, what is a "legal fiction"? According to the *Concise Law
Dictionary*, [1] a legal fiction is "a statement or supposition which is
known to be untrue, but which is not allowed to be denied in order
that some difficultly may be overcome," Maine, in his *Ancient
Law* [2] uses the term "legal fiction" in a wider sense to include
"any assumption which conceals or affects to conceal that a rule of
law has undergone alteration, its letter remaining unchanged and
its operation being modified."

An example of a legal fiction in its more narrow sense from

---

1 Osborn (Sweet & Maxwell, 1964) p. 6.
2 1863, p. 25.

Roman Law is the *"manumission per vindictum,"* which was a method whereby a slave could become free. It was "a fictitious suit, in which a person claimed that a slave was freeborn. The master admitted the claim and the magistrate made a decree establishing the freedom of the slave." [3]

The imagination of the English jurists was equally fertile when with the increase of international trade the limits of territorial jurisdiction presented difficulties. "In order to meet the difficulty of contracts made beyond the seas a fiction was adopted ... the Writ alleged that the contract was a transaction made or entered into, according to the custom of merchants at the place where it was made e.g. at Marseilles and proceeded to add *"Apud Mary-le-Bow in Cheapside"* or some other venue within the jurisdiction of the Common Law Courts." [4]

SECTION I

LEGAL FICTIONS AND *HA'ARAMOT* DISTINGUISHED

The *"Ha'aramah"* (translated "artifice") frequently met with in the Talmud closely resembles the legal fiction. It will be argued in this chapter, however, that frequently the *Ha'aramah* in Jewish Law was not used "in order that some difficulty may be overcome," or in order to conceal a change in the established law, but often on the contrary, in circumstances where there was a danger of the established law being confused or forgotten, and the *Ha'aramah* was brought into play as a guard against that potential risk.

---

3 Hunter, *Introduction to Roman Law* (Sweet & Maxwell, 1908) p. 23.
4 Potter, *Historical Introduction to English Law* (1958) p. 207.

Ha'aramot which do not circumvent the Law

The following examples of *Ha'aramah* will illustrate this argument :

In *Massekhet Shabbat,* [5] the Talmud considers what is to happen when an animal and its offspring have fallen down a well on *Yom Tov.* An animal cannot be moved on *Yom Tov,* because of the rabbinic laws of *Mukzeh,* [6] unless it is required for its meat, in which case it may be handled for the purpose of slaughter. If this had been a case where only one animal had fallen down the well, the solution would have been a simple one. The animal could have been raised for the purpose of slaughter. In this case, however, there is a complication. The Torah prohibits the slaughter of an animal and its offspring on one and the same day, [7] and so it is not possible to raise both animals from the well for the purpose of slaughter. Consequently, R. Joshua suggests the following artifice, "Let him first raise one of the animals from the well in order to slaughter it and then not slaughter it. [8] He then raises the next animal, in order to slaughter that and he can, in fact, slaughter whichever one he likes." [9]

In this type of case, there is, in fact, an element of fiction. True, it is prescribed that the owner must, as he raises the animal, have the intention of slaughtering it. However, the "intention" is in conflict with his knowledge that he will change his mind.

In this case the *Ha'aramah* was not instrumental in effecting any

5 *Shabbat* 117B.
6 See *ante* p. 63 Note 21.
7 Lev. XXII, 28.
8 Rashi explains, that he can make an excuse that he would rather see the other animal in case it is fatter.
9 There are a number of similar cases. See *Shabbat* 117B, "Saving property from fire." *Bezah* 11B, "Salting meat on *Yom Tov.*" *Pesahim* 46A, "Taking *Halla* when ritually unclean."

change in the law or overcoming any difficulty in the law. Here
the position was that an animal was in distress, and the Torah expressly prohibits the causing of pain and distress to animals. Accordingly, the fundamental position in law is that the prohibition
of *Mukzeh* does not apply to the case where an animal has to be
handled in order to alleviate its distress. [10] However, R. Joshua
requires the *Ha'aramah* as a reminder that in normal circumstances
an animal must not be handled on a *Yom Tov*, except for slaughter.

Our next example is from *Massekhet Mo'ed-Katan*, [11] where
R. Judah rules that a scribe may write and sell *Tefillin* and *Mezuzot* during the mid-festival (*Hol-Hamo'ed*) provided he had originally intended them for his own use. He can, in fact, continually
write *Tefillin* and *Mezuzot* for his own use and continually change
his mind and sell them.

Here again, there is an element of fiction. As in the previous
case, so here the "intention" of the scribe to use the *Tefillin* for
himself is in conflict with the "knowledge" that he will change his
mind. And here again, the *Ha'aramah* plays no part in the legal
process which in effect permits the scribe to write *Tefillin* and
Mezuzot for sale. Fundamentaly, the prohibition against writing
for business purposes on *Hol-Hamo'ed* does not apply to the trade
of a scribe who writes religious scrolls. [12] R. Judah requires the
Ha'aramah however, as a reminder that under normal circumstances it is an infringement of the laws of *Hol Hamo'ed* to write for
business purposes.

It hardly requires to be pointed out that in any event the
somewhat unreal "intention" in the two cases cited is a far cry
from the complete fabrication involved in the legal fictions of
Roman and English Law, like the affirmation that Marseilles is in

---

10   See Maimonides, *Yom Tov* II, 4.
11   **Moed-Katan* 19A.
12   This is R. Jose's view, but he requires no *Ha'aramah*.

Bow or that a slave is a freeman. "Intentions" in the sense of unspoken thoughts have no legal effect in Jewish Law [13] and in any event, the intention in the sense of "purpose" of an act is of necessity hard to nail down. Judge Silberg, for example, describes [14] as a legal fiction the *Ha'aramah* of R. Tarfon, [15] who in time of famine married three hundred women so that, he being a priest, they as wives of a priest would be able to eat *Trumah* which was plentiful. We find it difficult to see why marrying a poor woman to save her from starving should be any more fictitious than marrying a rich woman to prevent oneself from starving. The "intention" or "purpose" is more noble in the one case than in the other, but does that render the marriage more fictitious?

The Pruzbal

Our final example is Hillel's famous *"Pruzbal"*. The Talmud [16] states that when Hillel found that people were not lending money to those in need, for fear that the debts would be remitted in the Sabbatical year, [17] he ordained the *Pruzbal*. This was a document which the creditor made out and which stated that he handed over his debt to the *Bet Din* for collection. Once this document had been executed the debts were no longer remitted in the Sabbatical year.

This *Pruzbal* is considered a classical case of legal fiction, because there is a pretence that the debt has been assigned to *Bet Din*, when in fact, nothing of the sort had taken place.

In fact, however, here again the *Ha'aramah* of *Pruzbal* plays

13 *Kiddushin* 49B *"Debarim She-belev einam debarim."*
14 *Kakh Darko Shel Talmud* (Jerusalem, 1964) p. 26.
15 *Jerus. Yebamot* IV, 12.
16 **Gittin* 36A.

no part in the process which permits the debt to be recovered after the Sabbatical Year. This is made clear in the Talmud. The Talmud [16] asks : "Has Hillel the power to abolish the laws applicable to the Sabbatical Year?" and Raba replies that, in fact, the Sabbatical Year continues to operate and so remit all debts. [17] However, Hillel had made use of the power vested in the *Bet Din* to expropriate property when public policy required this. By virtue of this power, Hillel has expropriated the amount of the debt in the possession of the debtor and restored it to the lender. [18]

It will be noted that the *Pruzbal* played no part in this "expropriation." The power of expropriation had been enjoyed by every *Bet Din* since the days of Sinai [19] and required neither *Pruzbal* nor any document or formality for its operation. The *Pruzbal* was instituted, however, so that it should not be forgotten, in those circumstances, that the Torah had provided for the remission of debts in the Sabbatical Year. [20]

In fact, not all cases of *Ha'aramah* conform to this pattern. There are a number of cases where the *Ha'aramah* is not imposed

17 See Deut. XV, 1-2 "at the end of every seven years thou shalt make a remission and this is the manner of the remission, every lender that lendeth ought unto his fellow shall remit it, he shall not exact it of his fellow."

18 This is the view of Rashi, *ad. loc.*, but see Tosefot.

19 K. Kahana Kagan writes: "The right of expropriation by courts and communal leaders was incontestable. Maimonides summarises the general Rabbinic view by saying that a judge may always expropriate money belonging to whom whatsoever, destroy it and give it away, if in his judgment this would serve to prevent the breaking down of defences of the law or to strengthen its structure... This was one of the instruments for elasticity of the law. It was not the Rabbis themselves, however, who created this right of expropriation. They found source for it in the Bible." *Three Great Systems of Jurisprudence* (Stevens & Sons, 1955). p. 160.

20 In the previous two illustrations our interpretation of *Ha'aramah* is a tentative suggestion. In this case, however, this is how the *Ha'aramah* must be interpreted, if Rashi's view is followed.

in order to protect the normal law, but as a device which "enables some difficulty to be overcome or which allows the letter of the law to remain unchanged and its operation to be modified." Some of these cases will be discussed next. It will be noted that even in these cases there is no fictional pretence that something has taken place "which is not allowed to be denied." On the contrary, both law and fact are strictly observed in the cases which will be considered. Some say they are too strictly upheld; so much so that the spirit of the law is destroyed and the purpose of the law vitiated.

SECTION II

THE LAW AND THE REASONS FOR THE LAW

Do the many cases of *Ha'aramah* which are known to the Talmud destroy the spirit of the law? Why did the Sages not legislate to close loopholes in the law? Perhaps they did not originate the *Ha'aramot*, but why did they not put an end to them? These and similar questions have all been asked in connection with such *Ha'aramot* as conform strictly with the letter of the law, but which seem to vitiate the very result which the law was intended to produce.

Ha'aramot which circumvent the Law

Before attempting to answer these questions, let us consider some illustrations of this type of *Ha'aramah*. One such *Ha'aramah* is that which concerns tithe. In connection with tithe the Talmud [1]

1 *Berakhot* 31A.

suggests that since the obligation to give tithe arises only at the time when corn which has been winnowed is brought in by the front gate, it is possible to bring the corn by the front gate *before* it has been winnowed, or not to bring it into the *front gate* at all, and so escape the liability for tithe altogether.

In another case, the *Mishnah* [2] suggests a method of overcoming the task of carrying *Maaser Sheni* to Jerusalem, without any additional expense. Normally, a person was entitled to redeem his own *Maaser Sheni* and take the money to Jerusalem instead. If he did this, he had to add one-fifth of its value. [3] One is also entitled to redeem another person's *Maaser Sheni,* and in that case there is no need to add a fifth. The Sages say "a man may say to his son and daughter ... 'here is money — you redeem the *Maaser Sheni,'* " by so doing, he can save himself the liability for the additional one-fifth.

If a poor man has made a vow not to derive any benefit from his benefactor and now finds that he has nothing to eat, the Sages say that the benefactor can give some food to a friend who may then pass it on to the poor man. [4]

The Mishnah [5] states that "one may not derive benefit from *Hamez* which belongs to a Jew and which had been in his possession over Passover." *Hamez* belonging to a Gentile is not prohibited for it is written (Exod. XIII, 17). "Let it not be seen of *thee."* Now, states the *Tosefta,* if "a Jew and a Gentile travel in a ship and the Jew has *Hamez* in his possession, he can sell it to the Gentile and buy it back after Passover." [6]

---

2   *Maaser-Sheni* IV, 4.
3   Leviticus XXVII, 31.
4   *Nedarim* V, 6.
5   *Pesahim* II, 2.
6   The sale must be an outright sale, *Tosefta Pesahim* II, 6. See also *Orah Hayyim* 448, 3 and *Mekor Hayyim, loc. cit.* 11.

Purpose in Law

These then are the types of *Ha'aramot* which rightly or wrongly have been described as "legal fictions" and which have given rise to the question why the Sages permitted these devices, which, while paying homage to the letter of the law, were designed to frustrate its purpose and spirit.

We would suggest that the answer is that Torah law is essentially different from other systems of law. It is inappropriate to speak glibly of destroying the purpose and spirit of the Torah Law, because, as will be shown, the reason or purpose of a law of the Torah is hardly ever certain and frequently entirely unknown. In such circumstances, it is not possible to speak of destroying the *spirit* — in the sense of the "purpose" — of a law.

The laws of the Torah are divided into two categories: one, "*Hukkim,*" whose purpose cannot be understood, and the other, "*Mishpatim,*" whose purpose appears self-evident. Yet even there it must not be thought that one's own rationalisation explains God's purpose. The *Mishnah* states in *Massekhet Megillah* [7] that one must not refer in prayer to God's command to send away the mother bird before taking eggs from a nest, by saying "your mercy extends to a bird's nest." The Talmud explains that it is wrong to say so, because God's commands are absolute decrees and not attributed to "mercy." [8]

Even where the reason for a law is clear, the Sages held that

7 *Megillah 25A, Berakhot 33B.
8 See Asriel Rosenfeld, *Intercom* Vol. III, No. 3.

the law is not governed by its purpose. [9] For example, when the Torah speaks of the seven tribes which inhabited Canaan and states, "Neither shalt thou intermarry with them for they will turn away thy sons... that they may serve other gods." R. Simeon argues [10] that this text must be construed as prohibiting all intermarriage, not only intermarriage with the seven tribes, because any marriage out of the faith presents the same danger. The Sages, however, did not heed this argument, they considered that the law cannot be governed by its purpose. These particular words of the Bible were directed against the seven tribes and must remain limited in that manner, although if one were to consider their purpose, all intermarriage should be brought within the ambit of the prohibition. [11]

Strict interpretation

In view of what has been said, it is not possible to complain that *Ha'aramot* give rise to a too strict or literal interpretaion of the law and to claim that an interpretation in accordance with the

---

9 In fact, the Sages stated that the Torah itself makes it clear that God's commands are not governed by their purpose. This is shown clearly by God's command at Sinai that all men must stay away from their wives for three days before the Torah was given (Exodus IX, 15). The purpose of this command was to make certain that the men would be ritually clean on that great day. After the Torah had been given, the purpose of the command had been spent and, therefore, if God's command were governed by its purpose, the men would have been entitled to return to their women without any further word from God. Here it is seen that the laws of the Torah are not governed by their purpose, because, in fact, a further command from God was issued after the Torah had been given (Deut. V, 27), "Let them return to their tent" *Bezah* 5A, and see Rashi, *"Mino"* and Tosefot *"Mechdo."*

10 *Kiddushin 68B.

11 The Sages, in fact, agree that all intermarriage is prohibited, but they deduce it from a different text.

so called "spirit" of the law is called for. True, normally a law can be interpreted either strictly or in accordance with the purpose it was intended to serve. Where, however, as in most Torah laws, the latter possibility is ruled out, there is no alternative but to construe the law strictly.

Indeed there are endless examples of the law being construed in the strictest sense, even outside the realm of *Ha'aramah*. For example. the rule discussed in *Massekhet Ketubot* [12] "that a widow who has returned to her father's house after her husband's death must claim her *Ketuba* within twenty-five years." "Does it, then depend on this?" asks the Talmud, "If she claims, before sunset at the end of the 25 years, she gets her *Ketuba*, and if after sunset, she forfeits it?" "Yes", is the answer given and the Talmud goes on to explain that there are many cases in which the law is applied with equal stringency. In fact, examples can be supplied almost without limit.

One minute before night on Saturday, anyone who kindles fire or chops wood and so on, has committed a capital offence, one minute later, these acts can be done with impunity.

Forty *seah* of water constitute a proper *Mikveh;* one drop less and the *Mikveh* has no power of ritual purification.

A ring worth one *prutah* passing from a man to a woman is a sufficient gift in a valid marriage ceremony. [13] If the ring is worth only a tenth of a *prutah* less, the ceremony has no legal effect.

The law, then, is strictly interpreted in all these cases; and it is to be strictly interpreted, even if, as a result of strict interpretation, the obligation imposed by the law upon the individual becomes less onerous.

12   *Ketubot* 104A.
13   *Kiddushin* I, 1.

It would be quite wrong, where the intention of the law is un-known; to invent an "intention" or "purpose" for a *Mizvah* and then object to an *Ha'aramah* on the ground that it defeats the purpose one has invented.

To revert to the *Ha'aramah* of selling *Hamez* to a non-Jew over Passover and purchasing it back after Passover: this, as has been said, is based upon the law that only *Hamez* belonging to a Jew which had remained in existence over Passover is prohibited, but *Hamez* belonging to a non-Jew which had remained in existence over Passover in permitted. If it were certain that the Torah has some objection to the very existence of *Hamez* over Passover, and yet confines its prohibition to *Hamez* in the possession of Jews only because it legislates for Jews only, then the *Ha'aramah* of selling *Hamez* to a non-Jew and buying it back after Passover would be open to the objection that it destroys the spirit of the law. Since, however there is nothing to indicate that the Torah objects to *Hamez* as such, it is absurd to invent a purpose for this law and then to protest that the selling of *Hamez* defeats the purpose so invented.

This argument, however, must not be carried to too great a length. It must not be claimed that only the letter and not the spirit of the law is important.

Loopholes closed

Our purpose is to point out this difference between Torah law and other systems of law, and to make it clear that it is not always possible to think of the spirit of the law in connection with Torah, in the same terms as are relevant to other systems.

In fact, the Sages expressly disapproved of a number of *Ha'aramot,* presumably because they appreciated that these devices did, in fact, destroy the spirit of the law in the cases considered. [14]

Chajes [15] claims that the Sages did, in fact, consider that *Ha'ara-mot* are bad. However, according to Chajes, they were prepared to allow *Ha'aramot* in cases where there was a danger that the laws concerned would otherwise be transgressed. The Sages thought it better that the people should make use of loopholes than that they should transgress the law.

Presumably, then, where the Sages legislated to close loopholes, it was because they had no fear in the particular case that the law would be transgressed. For, as has been said, there were occasions when the Sages enacted laws to close loopholes.

For example, the Sages enacted a law which made corn liable for tithe, even where it had been winnowed by a non-Jew. This law was enacted when the Sages discovered that wealthy people transferred their corn to a non-Jew, so that it could be winnowed while in his ownership and so escape the incidence of tithe. [16]

They also enacted that an ox castrated by a non-Jew could not be retained by a Jew. This was because they found that owners were so arranging matters that their oxen should be castrated by a non-Jew. [17]

They also enacted legislation making unrolled dough liable for *Ḥallah,* because people were making use of a loophole in the law

---

14 In the case of *"Heter Iska"* which enables one to charge interest on a loan (contrary to Levit. XXV, 35) by declaring it to be in the nature of a partnership venture. It has been said that although the *Heter Iska* can be used whatever the nature of the loan, it would be wrong to make use of it, in order to take interest on a loan to a poor person. On the other hand, in connection with a commercial loan, why should a lender allow a large commercial enterprise to wax even bigger on his finance if he can charge interest through the medium of a *Heter Iska*?

15 *Darkey Hahoraah* II.

16 *Menaḥot 67A and see Rashi, *ad. loc.*

17 *Baba Meẓia 90A.

which made dough liable for *Hallah* only after it had been rolled. [18]

It is clear, therefore, that *Ha'aramot* were not always over-looked, nor were they always prohibited. The reaction of the Sages depended on the individual case, and whether or not in the judgment of the Sages the sanctity of the law concerned was imperilled.

18 *Jerus. Hallah* III, 1.

HEBREW SOURCES

SECTION I

HA'ARAMOT WHICH SERVE AS A REMINDER OF THE LAW

5. *Shabbat* 117B

אותו ואת בנו שנפלו לבור רבי אליעזר אומר מעלה את הראשון על מנת לשוחטו והשני עושה לו פרנסה במקומו בשביל שלא ימות. רבי יהושע אומר מעלין את הראשון על מנת לשוחטו ואינו שוחטו, ומערים ומעלה את השני רצה זה שוחט רצה זה שוחט.

11. *Moed Katan* 19A

ת״ר כותב אדם תפילין ומזוזות לעצמו, וטווה על יריכו תכלת לציציתו ולאחרים בטובה דברי רבי מאיר, ר' יהודה אומר מערים ומוכר את שלו וחוזר וכותב לעצמו. ר' יוסי אומר כותב ומוכר כדרכו כדי פרנסתו.

16. *Gittin* 36A

תנן התם פרוסבול אינו משמט, זה אחד מן הדברים שהתקין הלל הזקן, שראה את העם שנמנעו מלהלוות זה את זה, ועברו על מה שכתוב בתורה ״השמר לך פן יהיה דבר עם לבבך בליעל וגו׳״ (דברים ט״ז) עמד והתקין פרוסבול. וזה הוא גופו של פרוסבול מוסרני לכם פלוני דייני שבמקום פלוני שכל חוב שיש לי אצל פלוני שאגבנו כל זמן שארצה, והדיינים חותמים למטה או העדים. ומי איכא מידי דמדאורייתא משמטא שביעית והתקין הלל דלא משמטא ? אמר אביי בשביעית בזמן הזה ורבי היא. (והלל כרבי סבירא ליה דאמר שביעית להשמטת מלוה בזמן הזה דרבנן הוא — רש״י). רבא אמר הפקר ב״ד היה הפקר.

SECTION II

HA'ARAMOT WHICH CONFORM WITH THE LETTER OF THE LAW

1. *Berakhot* 31A

מערים אדם על תבואתו ומכניסה במוץ שלה כדי שתהא בהמתו אוכלת
ופטורה מן המעשר.

2. *Maaser Sheni* IV, 4

מערימין על מעשר שני, כיצד ? אומר אדם לבנו ולבתו הגדולים, לעבדו
ולשפחתו העברים, "הילך מעות אלה ופדה לך מעשר שני זה". אבל לא יאמר כן
לבנו ולבתו הקטנים ולעבדו ולשפחתו הכנענים מפני שידן כידו.

4. *Nedarim* V, 6

המודר הנאה מחבירו. ואין לו מה יאכל, נותנו לאחר לשום מתנה והלה
מותר בה.

6. *Tosefta Pesaḥim* II, 6

ישראל ונכרי, שהיו באין בספינה וחמץ ביד ישראל הרי זה מוכרו לנכרי
ונותנו במתנה וחוזר ולוקח ממנו לאחר הפסח. ובלבד שיתנו לו במתנה גמורה.

THE LAW AND ITS REASON OR PURPOSE

7. *Megillah* 25A

מתני׳ : האומר ... על קן ציפור יגיעו רחמיך ... משתקין אותו :
גמ׳ : מ״ט ...מפני שעושה מדותיו של הקב״ה רחמים ואינן אלא גזירות.

10. *Kiddushin* 66B and 68B

מתני׳ : וכל מי שאין לה לא עליו ולא על אחרים קידושין הולד כמותה ואיזה
זה ולד שפחה ונכרית :

גמ׳ : נכרית מנלן ? אמר קרא ״לא תתחתן בם״ (דברים ז׳). אשכחנא דלא
תפסי בה קידושי ולדה כמותה מנלן ? א״ר יוחנן משום ר״ש בן יוחי דאמר
קרא ״כי יסיר את בנך מאחרי״ בנך הבא מישראלית קרוי בנך ואין
בנך הבא מן העובדת כוכבים קרוי בנך אלא בנה......ההוא בשבעה גוים

כתיב! שאר אומות מנלן? א"ק "כי יסיר את בנך" לרבות כל המסירים.
הניחא לר"ש דדריש טעמא דקרא אלא לרבנן מ"ט?

THE LAW IS STRICTLY INTERPRETED

12. *Ketubot* 104A

מתני'... וחכ"א כל זמן שהיא בבית בעלה גובה כתובתה לעולם כל זמן
שהיא בבית אביה גובה כתובתה עד עשרים וחמש שנים.

גמ': אמר ליה אביי לרב יוסף אתאי שקיעת החמה גובה כתובתה,
לאחר שקיעת החמה לא גביא, בההיא פורתא אחילתא? א"ל אין, כל מדת
חכמים כן היא בארבעים סאה טובל בארבעים סאה חסר קורטוב אינו יכול
לטבול בהן.

LOOPHOLES WHICH WERE CLOSED

16. *Menaḥot* 67A

והא האי תנא דאמר מירוח העכו"ם אינו פוטר, גלגול העכו"ם פוטר?
מדרבנן, גזירה משום בעלי כיסים. (שיש להם קרקעות הרבה וחסים על רוב
מעשרות ויקנוהו לעכו"ם וימריחום עכו"ם ומפקע ליה ממעשר (רש"י).

17. *Baba Mezia* 90A

ת"ש דשלחו ליה לאבוה דשמואל הלין תורי דגנבין ארמאי ומגנחין יתהון
(ומסרסין אותם ואח"כ מחזירין לבעלים ומאהבת בעליו ישראל גונבו הנכרי —
רש"י) מהו? שלח להו הערמה אתעביד בהו אערימו עלייהו ויזדבנון.

18. *Jerus. Hallah* III, 1

אוכלין עראי מן העיסה עד שתגלגל.
אמר ר' חגיי לא שנו אלא עראי אבל קבע אסור. מפני שהוא מערים לפוטרה
מן החלה.

CHAPTER VI

THE MISHNAH OF THE SAGES

THE MISHNAH OF THE SAGES

INTRODUCTION

No discussion of the contribution made by the Sages to the Oral Law is complete without a reference to their work in connection with the *Mishnah*. The *Mishnah* is the basis of the Oral Law which is known to us, and its formulation was entirely the work of the Sages. There is no suggestion that the text of the *Mishnah* is of divine origin. What, in fact, is its origin? In this chapter, we will discuss various views regarding the origin and purpose of the *Mishnaic* arrangement.

Midrashic and Mishnaic Styles distinguished

The *Mishnah* normally comprises a simple statement of the law or of a difference of Rabbinic opinion concerning the law and it does not make any reference to the Scripture. For example, the *Mishnah*[1] states "Fifteen women render their co-wives ... free from Levirate marriage." This statement is in the *Mishnaic* style, and does not adduce any Scriptural proof. Occasionally, a *Mishnah*

---

1 *Yebamot* I, 1.

will refer to the Scriptural passage on which it is based,[2] it is then said to be in *Midrashic* style. The *Sifra* and *Sifrei* are entirely in *Midrashic* style; the *Mishnah*, on the other hand, as the name suggests is almost entirely in *Mishnaic* style.

Which came first?

R. Sherira Gaon, (10th Century) head of the Academy in Pumbedita, in a passage contained in his famous letter addressed to the community at Kairawan, remarks *"Sifra* and *Sifrei* are *drash* on the Scripture ... and in the early times, in the days of the Second Temple, in the days of the early masters, this was the method of learning."[3] From this statement it appears that the *Midrashic* style of the *Sifra* and *Sifrei* preceded the *Mishnaic* style, and it has been thought accordingly that the origin of the *Mishnah* is to be found in *Midrashic* statements of law.[4] For example, the *Mishnah* which we have quoted may have originated from a *Midrashic* text in the following form: "Fifteen women render their co-wives ... free from Levirate marriage ... as it is written, (Lev. XVIII, 18) 'Neither shalt thou take a wife to her sister to vex her.' " Later the *Midrashic* statement of *Halachah* was stripped of its scriptural proof and became known as a *Mishnah*. Those who write about this change of style claim that the change took place at about the time when the *Tannaim* embarked upon the first arrangement of the *Mishnah*. This leads us to the first problem to be discussed in this chapter "when did the first arrangement of the *Mishnah* take place?"

---

2 For instance: *Nega'im* XII, 5 *et. seq.; Sotah* VIII, 1, 2; *Yebamot* XII, 6; *Sanhedrin* I, 4 *et. seq.* II, 4, IV, 5, VI, 2 *et. seq.*

3 *Igeret Rav Sherira Gaon,* Edition Hyman (London, 1910, Jerusalem, 1967) p. 39.

4 See for instance D.Z. Hoffman, *Die Erste Mischna.*

SECTION I

THE FIRST *MISHNAH* ARRANGEMENT

(i) *The Time of Yabneh*

Various passages of the Talmud and of other early writings have been said to provide a clue to the period when the first arrangement of the *Mishnah* took place, and it may be rewarding to examine some of these passages in detail. We shall consider in all the evidence produced in support of five different periods (not taken in chronological order).

Firstly, we turn to the *Tosefta* in *Eduyot*. [5] This states that "when the Sages entered *Kerem B'Yabneh* they said, "A time will come when a man will seek a matter from the words of the Torah and not find it, from the words of the Scribes and not find it ... No one thing of the Torah will be like the other" and as a result they embarked upon an arrangement of the *Mishnayot* of Hillel and Shammai.

It has been said [6] that this passage indicates the concern the Sages felt for the future of the Oral Law in the absence of any systematic arrangment of *Mishnayot*. It follows from this that at the time of Yabneh, there was no such arrangement.

It also follows that *Massekhet Eduyot*, which was then produced, was the beginning of the first collection of *Mishnayot*.

It is, however, questionable whether this is the correct interpretation of the *Tosefta*. [7] Moreover, if the Sages were, in fact,

---

5   **Eduyot* I, 1.
6   Albeck, *Mabo L'Mishnah* (Jerusalem, 1959) p. 82.
7   See *infra.* p. 155.

concerned about the need for a *Mishnah* arrangement they would not have sought the remedy in an arrangement like *Massekhet Eduyot,* which classifies *Mishnayot* according to the *Tannaim* whose statements are recorded. Such a classification could not have got very far at a time when most *Mishnayot* were anonymous.

(ii) The Time of R. Akiba

It is necessary to consider next a dictum in *Massekhet Sanhedrin* [8] that, "Whenever an anonymous opinion is stated in the *Mishnah* it is that of R. Meir, in the *Tosefta* that of R. Nehemiah, in the *Sifra* that of R. Judah and in the *Sifrei* that of R. Simeon, and they all follow R. Akiba."

On the basis of this dictum, it has been suggested [9] that R. Akiba is responsible for the first *Mishnah* arrangement, that he was the first to organize *Halachot* in a logical manner, and that the other *Tannaim* who are said to "follow R. Akiba" followed his example in their collection of *Halachot.* It will be realized that this passage from *Massekhet Sanhedrin* is capable of more than one interpretation. [10] Moreover, the same may be said of an *Aggadic* passage, which had similarly been claimed to refer to R. Akiba's work of arranging *Mishnayot.* [11] The *Aggadah* concerned likens R. Akiba "to a worker who takes his basket and goes out to find corn and collects it in his basket. He finds oat and puts them in, spelt and puts them in etc. When he enters his house, he sorts out the wheat separately and the spelt separately." [12]

8   *Sanhedrin* 86A.
9   Frankel, *Darkhey Hamishnah* (Tel-Aviv, 1959) p. 15.
10   See *infra* p. 151.
11   Frankel *op. cit.* p. 221.
12   *Abot D'Rabbi Natan* XVIII, 1.

(iii) The Time of Bet Shammai and Bet Hillel

A much earlier period for the first arrangement of the *Mishnah* is suggested by a Responsa in *Sha'arey Teshubah*. [13] There we read as follows "You should know that from the days of Moses our teacher to Hillel the Elder there were six hundred orders of the *Mishnah* [14] that were given by God to Moses at Sinai. From Hillel onwards the world became impoverished and diminished and the glory of the Torah weakened and from Hillel and Shammai they produced no more than six orders."

It has been said [15] on the basis of this text that the *Mishnah* was first arranged at the time of Bet Hillel and Bet Shammai. Combining this with the statement of Sherira Gaon [16] that at about that time *Halachot* ceased to be presented in *Midrashic* style, the conclusion is reached that the arrangement of the *Mishnah* and the changing of the form of *Halachic* texts were really part and parcel of the same venture undertaken in the time of Bet Shammai and Bet Hillel.

(iv) The Time of the Men of the Great Synagogue

There is, however, one view which suggests an even earlier period for the first *Mishnah* arrangement. It is not based on any external evidence, but on the text of the *Mishnah* itself. We are referring to the view of Halevy, [17] who looks to the period of the

---

13   **Sha'arey Teshubah* I, 20.
14   See also *Hagigah* 14A for reference to 600 orders of the Mishnah.
15   Hoffmann, *op. cit.*
16   *ante* p. 144.
17   *Dorot Harishonim Part I, Volume 3. p. 206.

Men of the Great Synagogue for the first complete *Mishnah* arrangement.

He argues as follows: All disputes between *Tannaim* which are reported in the Mishnah concern some point arising out of a *principle* which has been stated either in the same or in a previous *Mishnah*. The *Tannaim* never dispute or refute this principle but they invariably argue about its application in detail only. It follows that the statement of principle preceded the argument of the *Tannaim* in point of time. This statement of principle which may be called *"Yesod Hamishnah"* is part of an original *Mishnah* collection which covers all the principles of the Oral Law. [18] There are no disputes

---

18 It will be useful to analyse two *Mishnayot* in accordance with Halevy's theory. (In the following two *Mishnayot*, the *Yesod Hamishnah* is given in italics.)

Mishnah I "If a corpse lay in a room to which there are many entrances they are all unclean... If there was intention to take the corpse, out through one of them, this affords protection to all other entrances. Bet Shammai say the intention must have been formed before the corpse was dead, Bet Hillel say it is enough if the intention was formed after it was dead" (*Oholot* VII, 3).

The *Yesod* here lays down the undisputed principle: the argument centres round the word "intention" in that principle i.e. at what point of time must the *intention* have been present?

Mishnah II "A woman is acquired by three ways... by money, by writ or by intercourse. By money, Bet Shammai say by a *Dinar*... and Bet Hillel say by a *Prutah"* (*Kiddushin* I, 1).

Again the *Yesod* lays down the general principle and the argument concerns the amount of "money."

Albeck criticises Halevy for failing to distinguish between an old law and an old *Mishnah* text. He says that the fact that Bet Shammai and Bet Hillel and later *Tannaim* often argue concerning details of a principle set out in the *Yesod Hamishnah* does not prove that the text of the *Yesod* is of early origin. It merely shows that the principle of law contained in the *Yesod*, i.e. the subject matter of the *Mishnayot* is of long standing.

According to Albeck, *Mishnah* I shows merely that the extent to which a corpse spreads its uncleanness was well established long before the time of Bet Shammai and Bet Hillel and *Mishnah* II shows the

concerning these principles, as distinct from their application in detail. Since there are no disputes, we must conclude that the *Yesod Hamishnah* dates back to the period of the Men of the Great Synagogue when there was a Sanhedrin and "there were no disputes in Israel." The *Sanhedrin*, of course, continued to function down to the time of Hillel and Shammai, but after the period of the Men of the Great Synagogue conditions in the land were so unsettled that no *Halachic* work of any major importance could have been undertaken.

If this idea of *Yesod Hamishnah* is accepted, then it will be discovered that frequently the *Yesod Hamishnah* is in *Mishnaic* style and the disputes which are later additions to it are in

same regarding the requirement of money in a marriage contract. There is, however, no proof that these principles existed in the form of an established *Mishnah* text. Bet Hillel and Bet Shammai did not have before them a general arrangement of the *Mishnah,* but a number of old laws which were well established in their time, and which had not yet assumed a settled text. These laws might be expressed variously by the different schools of the time: for example, while some taught "by three ways a woman is acquired etc." others taught "a man acquires a woman by etc." and yet others "a contract of marriage is concluded by a man giving to a woman etc." Albeck *op cit.* p. 65 and 82.

Professor Rabbi J. J. Weinberg, *Samuel Mirsky Jubilee Volume* (N.Y. 1958) however, comes to Halevy's support. He feels that a close textual analysis shows that the controversies between Bet Shammai and Bet Hillel in the cases referred to, concern not merely principles of law, but also the enunciation of those principles in a given text. He points out that in *Mishnah* II, the repetition of the words "by money" as an introduction to the controversy indicates that Bet Shammai and Bet Hillel were defining a term in a text, and in Mishnah I, the same is true of the word "intention".

Midrashic style. [19] This contradicts the findings previously discussed — that the *Midrashic* style preceded the *Mishnaic*. Halevy,[20] accordingly, is of the view that both styles together had long been in use, sometimes the one and sometimes the other.

(v) *The Time of R. Judah Hanasi*

Having discussed a view which puts the date of the first *Mishnah* arrangement as far back as possible, it is proposed to conclude with a view which goes to the other extreme and puts the date forward as far as possible. In this connection, we must

19 The following examples will illustrate this argument. (What Halevy calls the *Yesod Hamishnah* is in italics.)

   1. *If a man ate Trumah in error, he must pay its value plus one fifth* (*Terumot* VI, 1).

   R. Eliezar says "restitution may be made for one kind instead of another kind" ... R. Akiba says "restitution may be made only for the like kind." "And he shall give unto the priests the holy things" (Lev. XXII), "namely whatever is fit to be holy," says R. Eliezar. But R. Akiba says "the same kind of hallowed thing as he has eaten" (*Ibid.* VI, 6).

   2. *What counts as a defective cluster of grapes?* (*Olelot*). *Any cluster that lacks both shoulders and pendant* (*Peah* VII, 4).

   If a vineyard has only defective clusters, R. Eliezar says "they belong to the householder." R. Akiba says "they belong to the poor." R. Eliezar says "'When thou gatherest the grapes of thy vineyard thou shalt not take defective clusters' (Deut. XXIV). If there is no grape gathering, how can there be defective clusters?" R. Akiba said to him "'and from thy vineyard thou shalt not take defective clusters' (Lev. XIX) even if they are all defective clusters" ibid. VII, 7.

20 *op. cit.* Part I, Vol. 5 p. 543 *et. seq.* Halevy also points out that according to *Yebamot* 72B, R. Johanan had never studied the *Sifrey*. If the entire *Mishnah* is based on *Midrashic Halachot,* it is impossible that R. Johanan should have beeen ignorant of the most important *Midrash Halachah.*

again refer to the famous letter of Sherira Gaon where the problem under discussion is specifically raised. According to Sherira Gaon, before the time of R. Judah Hanasi they "did not have a generally accepted arrangement of the *Mishnah* in a uniform style and language. Although all the Sages were agreed on the substance of the oral tradition, everyone of them taught his pupils in whatever order or style he preferred." [21] There were different schools which taught identical principles, but they were taught in a variety of styles. R. Judah was the first to arrange the *Mishnah*. He did this by taking *Mishnayot* from the various schools — showing special preference for those which once came from the school of R. Meir [22] and arranging them in a logical order. [23]

SECTION II

THE PURPOSE OF THE MISHNAIC ARRANGEMENT

A Change in Style to Clarify the Law

In arranging the *Mishnah,* the endeavour of the Sages was not only the *classification* of the material of the Oral Law but also, as we shall try to show, the *clarification* of the law as it then stood. We

---

21 *op. cit. p. 28 et. seq.*
22 This is the usual interpretation of the passage from the Talmud *Sanhedrin* 86A quoted p. 146 *ante.*

Not all anonymous *Mishnayot* follow R. Meir: See *Ketubot* 71A, *Yebamot* 111B, *Baba Batra* 65B. The *Mishnah* of R. Simon Ish Hamizpe was chosen for *Massekhet Yoma* (Yoma 14B); that of R. Eliezar b. Jacob for *Massekhet Middot* (Yoma 16A); and that of R. Jose for *Massekhet Erubin* and *Massekhet Oholot* (*Erubin* 79A).

23 Those *Mishnayot* not included in the collection are known as *Baraita* "outside" texts.

would even suggest that the change which they made from the *Midrashic* to the *Mishnaic* style was motivated by their endeavour to clarify the laws. Firstly, however we shall mention three widely accepted theories which have been put forward to account for this change in style.

Three Theories

(i) The *Mishnaic* style was preferred, because it was easier to memorise. This would be an important consideration at a time when it was not permitted to reduce the Oral Law to writing.

(ii) With the increase of Rabbinic legislation, which does not rely on Scriptural proof, the *Midrashic* style was no longer suitable.

(iii) The *Midrashic* style was abandoned because it followed the arrangement of the law in the Pentateuch, and as the Pentateuch deals with different aspects of the identical topic in various places it was not possible to classify *Halachot* in order of subject matter while following the *Midrashic* manner of study. [1]

A New Theory

It may be, however, that the truth lies elsewhere: that the Sages endeavoured at the time of classification of the law also to achieve clarification of *Halachah* and that the *Midrashic* style was abandoned because it lacked the necessary authority. When a *Halachah* is stated to be derived from a scriptural passage, it is open to the argument that the passage concerned has been misinterpreted.

---

[1] These various theories have been put forward by writers from time to time. See Lauterbach, *Rabbinic Essays*.

The *Mishnaic* style, on the other hand, bears the hallmark of finality and the *Halachah* is stated beyond all argument. [2]

Two Eras of Clarification

The endeavour of the Sages to clarify Oral Law at the same time as they arranged it systematically is borne out by the two major arrangements of the *Mishnah* about which one can write with certainty. Although it has been seen that there is no general agreement on the question when the *first* arrangement of the *Mishnah* took place, it is beyond dispute that there was an arrangement of some *Mishnayot* at Yabneh and again at the time of R. Judah Hanasi.

Even R. Sherira Gaon, who declares that R. Judah Hanasi was the first "to arrange the *Halachah* so that the Rabbis should cite the law in a uniform language and style," [3] refers to the arrangement of *Messekhet Eduyyot* which took place in Yabneh generations earlier. [4]

---

2 This may explain Halevy's findings that the *Yesod Hamishnah* is frequently in *Mishnaic* style, whereas the argument of later *Tannaim* which follows is in *Midrashic* style. The *Mishnaic* passage represents a statement of established law which had accordingly been cast in *Mishnaic* style, whereas the *Midrashic* passage being more recent in origin had not yet undergone the process of change. See *Aboda Zara* 35A that the Palestinian Sages never disclosed their reason at the same time as they promulgated a *Gezerah*, because the *Gezerah* was more respected when its reason was not stated.

3 *op. cit.* p. 32.

4 He also refers to *Massekhet Ukzin* which was known in the time of R. Simon b. Gamliel (see Horiot 13B). *Massekhet Kelim* was known to R. Jose who knew how the *Massekhet* had been arranged, hence his statement (*Kelim* XXX, 4) "Blessed art thou O *Kelim* for thou didst enter in uncleanness but art gone forth in cleanness." See *Sefer Kritut*.

I. Yabneh

It will be shown in this chapter that both the generation of
Yabneh and that of R. Judah Hanasi had made it their concern to
see that the *Halachah* should be clearly stated and should speak
with a single voice. First let us deal with three indications that at
the time of Yabneh the Sages endeavoured to clarify the law.

(i) *Messekhet Eduyyot*

Messekhet Eduyyot speaks for the efforts made by the Sages
at Yabneh to clarify the law. It comprises, as its name suggests, the
"evidence" of the scholars regarding traditional rulings of law. It
also clarifies the law regarding the many disputes between Bet
Shammai and Bet Hillel. According to the Jerusalem Talmud, Yabneh was the place where a *Bat Kol* announced [5] that the rulings of
both Bet Shammai and Bet Hillel were "the words of the living
God" but that the rulings of Bet Hillel were law. [6]

(ii) *The Struggle with R. Eliezer*

R. Gamliel, the *Nasi* of that period, showed his determination
to assert a single unified *Halachic* authority. He even excommuni-
cated his colleague R. Eliezar when the latter refused to bow to the
Halachic ruling of the majority of Sages. R. Eliezar's ruling had the
support of a *Bat Kol*. [7] Nevertheless, he was told that the "Torah

5   *Jerus. Yebamot* I, "The *Bat-Kol* came at Yabneh."
6   *Erubin* 13B.
7   **Baba Meẓia* 59B.

was not in heaven" and the view of the majority of Sages must prevail. R. Gamliel explained his action in the following prayer:

"Sovereign of the Universe! Thou knowest full well that I have not acted for my honour nor for the honour of my parental house, but for Thine, so that strife may not multiply in Israel."

(iii) *The Struggle with R. Joshua*

R. Gamliel of Yabneh was determined that strife might not multiply in Israel, and that a unified *Halachic* authority should declare the law. When R. Joshua contradicted his authority on several occasions, R. Gamliel treated him with such severity that the people revolted on behalf of R. Joshua, and R. Gamliel had to step down from his high office. [8]

Yabneh was a time of comparative calm in the midst of political upheavals in the land, and the Sages felt that they must grasp the opportunity to establish the authority of *Halachah*. The urge to put an end to strife and to establish universally accepted *Halachic* rulings arose out of the concern of the Sages expressed in the *Tosefta* which has been cited earlier. [9] This *Tosefta* speaks of the fear the Sages had expressed at Yabneh that a time might come when a man would seek a clear ruling of *Halachah* without success. It has been seen that the concern of the Sages was attributed to the lack of a systematic arrangement of *Halachah*. It is more likely, however, what really worried the Sages was the uncertainty of the law caused by conflicting authority, because there would be no resemblance between the words of the Torah as expressed by Bet Shammai and the words of the Torah as expressed by Bet Hillel.

8   *Berakhot* 27B.
9   *ante, p. 145.

In organising the material of the Oral Law at Yabneh, the Sages, therefore, were mindful, not only of the need to produce a more convenient reference to the Oral Law, but also of the call for a more definite statement of the law as it stood.

II. R. Judah Hanasi

The redaction of the *Mishnah* by R. Judah Hanasi presents a similar pattern of classification and clarification. It has been said that "his great achievement in the days of finalising the *Mishnah* was that of deciding controversies which had remained unresolved since the days of Yabneh and turning such decisions into anonymous *Mishnayot*."[10] In this undertaking, R. Judah Hanasi was assisted by the members of his *Bet Din*.[11]

10 The following points should be made clear regarding anonymous Mishnayot:
   a. Anonymous *Mishnayot* are frequently the result of R. Judah Hanasi's work. See *Rosh Hashanah* 7B, *Ḥullin* 84A. The Talmud occasionally refers to anonymous Mishnayot as "here Rebbi learned." See *Giṭṭin* 29A.
   b. Not all anonymous *Mishnayot* are the result of Rebbi's work of deciding *Halachot*. Many *Mishnayot* had always been anonymous, because the law they state was never subject to any controversy.
   c. Sometimes, instead of presenting a decision of *Halachah* as an anonymous *Mishnah*, Rebbi presents it as the view of "the Sages."
   d. That the *Halachah* follows the anonymous *Mishnayot* is stated by R. Johanan *Shabbat* 46A, but see a general discussion of this proposition by S.K. Mirsky in *The Leo Jung Jubilee Volume* (New York) p. 155 *et. seq.*
11 *Oholot* XVIII, 9 and *Giṭṭin* V, 6. There are a number of instances in which Rebbi's view was defeated by a vote taken in the *Bet Din*. Consequently, there are anonymous *Mishnayot* which carry the rider that R. Judah took a different view of the law.

The Anonymous Mishnah

These anonymous *Mishnayot* clarified the law on *Halachic* problems which had been the subject of disputes. True that a law contained in an anonymous *Mishnah* may appear elsewhere in the *Mishnah* arrangement as still subject to a dispute. But there are rules for recognising the *Halachah* in such a case. Before these rules can be understood something has to be said about the *Mishnah* arrangement in general.

The Arrangement of Mishnayot

Whether the arrangement by R. Judah Hanasi is identical with that which is found in our present-day Mishnah is open to question. The six orders (*Sedarim*) as arranged at present, follow this sequence :

1. *Zeraim* (dealing mainly with the Laws of the Land of Israel and its fruit)
2. *Moed* (Laws of Sabbath and Holydays)
3. *Nashim* (Marriage and Divorce)
4. *Nezikin* (Torts)
5. *Kodoshin* (Laws relating to the Temple, its Objects and Sacrifices)
6. *Tohorot* (Laws of Ritual Purity)

It is, however, by no means certain that this is the arrangement which R. Judah Hanasi followed. While this arrangement is referred to in the Talmud, [12] the *Midrash* [13] knew of a different sequence of the order of the *Mishnah*.

12 R. Simeon b. Lakish. *Shabbat* 31A.
13 *Yalkut Tehilim* IX, The order there is *Nashim, Zeraim, Tohorot, Moed, Kodoshim* and *Nezikin.*

The origin of the sequence of *Massekhtot* within each *Seder* is similarly in doubt. While the *Talmud* provides an explanation why the *Sedarim* follow each other in the particular order mentioned, [14] the commentators have great difficulty in finding a rational explanation for the sequence in which the *Massekhtot* follow one another. In some respects, our present arrangement is quite extraordinary; there are such anomalies as the tractate dealing with divorce preceding that dealing with the laws of marriage.[15] It has been said [16] that the *Massekhtot* were arranged in order of size, with those having a greater number of chapters preceding those with lesser numbers. [17] However, this explanation is not completely satisfactory; *Seder Zeraim* does not follow that pattern.

14 It is said to follow Isaiah XXXIII, 6 "and there shall be faith (*Zeraim*) in thy time (*Moed*) a store (*Nashim*) of salvation (*Nezikin*) and wisdom (*Kodoshim*) and knowledge (*Tohorot*)."

15 R. Sherira Gaon (*op. cit.*) and Maimonides (*Introduction to Seder Zeraim*) have attempted to give some logical explanation for this apparent anomaly and also, for instance, why *Massekhet Sukkot* precedes *Massekhet Rosh Hashanah*. The explanation of Maimonides is of a homelitical nature and that of R. Sherira Gaon is incomplete in the available manuscripts. The first *Tosefot* in various *Massekhtot* are also concerned with this problem.

16 R. Margulies, *Yesod Hamishnah Vearikhatah* (Tel-Aviv, 1956), which also provides an explanation for the difficulty presented by *Seder Zeraim* in this connection.

17 This is certainly true for five of the six *Sedarim*. Note that originally the first three tractates of *Nezikin* formed a single *Massekhta* (*Baba Kama* 102A), as did also *Massekhtot Sanhedrin* and *Makkot* (Maimonides (*op. cit.*). Chapters 6 and 7 of *Messekhet Tamid* must be counted as one chapter, which is in accordance with some manuscripts (H. Strack, *Introduction to Talmud and Midrash*, p. 366 Note 14 (New York, 1959).

A Conflict between a Mishnah which is Anonymous and a Mishnah which is not

It is of importance to know whether, in fact, the present sequence of *Mishnayot* is identical with that which R. Judah Hanasi followed in his studies, because as has been stated there are cases where the identical statement of *Halachah* appears in two different *Mishnayot:* in one *Mishnah,* anonymously, and in another, as the statement of a particular *Tanna.*[18] In such cases, it is important to establish which of the two *Mishnayot* was studied first by R. Judah Hanasi, the anonymous one or that which reports the individual statement?[19] Because the rules for ascertaining the Halachah turn on the question which *Mishnah* was studied first by R. Judah Hanasi?

If of the two *Mishnayot* that which was first studied by R. Judah Hanasi is anonymous,[20] it is assumed that this expressed his first decision of *Halachah,* and that the second *Mishnah* indicates that he had later revoked this decision. If the second of two *Mishna-*

18 For example, *Sotah* IX, 1 states: "In the case of *Eglah Arufah* three Judges used to come from the Court in Jerusalem. R. Judah says five Judges." Here then the requirement of three Judges is stated anonymously. *Sanhedrin* I, 3 states: "The case of *Eglah Arufah* is decided upon by three Judges, says R. Simeon, R. Judah says five Judges." Here then the requirement of three Judges is reported as an individual view.

19 "The *Mishnah* which was studied last is the decisive one." *Yebamot* 42B, *Baba Kama* 102A, *Aboda Zara* 7A. *Niddah* 11B.

20 In the example given in Footnote 18, *Sotah* (in *Seder Nashim*) takes precedence over *Sanhedrin* (in *Seder Nezikin*) in the sequence of *Mishnayot,* so the *Halachah* requiring three Judges cannot be taken to have the support of R. Judah Hanasi, if the present order of the *Sedarim* is identical with that in which R. Judah Hanasi studied. See Rashbam, *Baba Batra* 122B, "Rebbi changed his mind."

yot is anonymous, it is assumed that R. Judah Hanasi had at first been uncertain and that the later *Mishnah* reflects his final decision. [21]

Sufficient has been said to show that the Sages who were responsible for the arrangement of the *Mishnah* were responsible also for producing some elementary form of codification. Were these same Sages also responsible for reducing the Oral Law to writing? Were these arrangements of the *Mishnah,* which have been discussed, handed down by word of mouth or had they been committed to writing? These questions remain to be considered.

SECTION III

THE WRITING OF THE *MISHNAH* AND THE CHARACTER OF THE SAGES

Was the First Mishnaic Arrangement in Writing or Oral?

There are many references in the Talmud to scrolls [1] and correspondence [2] in writing, concerning matters of *Halachah,* [3] notwith-

---

21 Rashi *Aboda Zara* 7A as explained by *Divrey Sofrim* (Jerusalem, 1956), Part I p. 77. According to R. Judah (*Baba Ḳama* 102A), it must be assumed that the present arrangement was that which R. Judah Hanasi followed in his studies where it concerns two *Mishnayot* in one *Massekhta.* When it comes however to two *Massekhot* or two different *Sedarim,* there are many different opinions. For a general discussion of the problem see **Tosefot Yom Tov, Sotah* IX, 1. See also *Kesef Mishneh, Hilchot Roẓeaḥ,* IX, 1; *Tosefot Shabbat* 81B and *Yebamot* 42B.

 1 *Megillat Taanit* (*Taanit* II, 8; *Erubin* 62B), *Megillat Yoḥsin* (*Yebamot* 49B),*Megillat Samamonim* (*Yoma* 38A).

 2 Letters from various Rabbis (*Shabbat* 116A, *Shabuot* 48B), a letter from Rabin (*Ketubot* 39A, *Baba Meẓia* 114A), thirty-nine camels loaded with letters from Samuel to R. Joḥanan (*Ḥulin* 95B).

 3 Concerning *Aggada* there is mention of a Book of *Aggada* (*Berakhot* 23A, *Baba Meẓia* 116A).

standing the prohibition against writing down Oral Law. [4] These written documents, however, were all for private use, [5] and the prohibition against writing down the Oral Law did not apply to these. [6] On the other hand, it is clear that the task of arranging the *Mishnah* had been undertaken in such a way as to achieve the maximum of publicity, because its purpose was "that all teachers should cite the law in a uniform language and style." [7] The *Mishnah* arrangement was therefore not for private use and it is unlikely that this arrangement was in writing, unless by that time the prohibition against the writing down of the Oral Law had been suspended.

From comments made by both Rashi [8] and the Tosefists, [9] it would appear that even by R. Judah's time, the prohibition against writing down the Oral Law for public study had not yet been lifted. Maimonides, [10] however, refers to "Rebbi who collected the traditional teachings and wrote them all down."

4 *Giṭṭin* 60B based on Exodus XXXIV, 27, "And the Eternal said unto Moses, 'Write thou these words, for according to these words have I made a covenant with thee and with Israel.'" From this the Sages deduced "what is said orally must not be stated in writing."
5 They may be identical with the "hidden scrolls" to which the Talmud (*Shabbat* 6A) refers.
6 "No text books were composed for *public teaching* of the Oral Law. However, the prophet or head of Bet Din of each generation would create notes for his own use of what he had heard from his teachers and would himself teach orally in public." Maimonides, *Introduction to Mishneh Torah.*
7 *Iggeret Sherira Gaon.*
8 See *Shabbat* 13B and *Erubin* 62B "nothing except *Megillat Taanit* had been reduced to writing" in the days of Abaye. See also *Baba Meẓia* 33A "later generations started writing it down."
9 *Megillah* 32A, Talmudists would chant the *Mishnah*, because it was not reduced to writing and the tune helped the memory.
10 *op. cit.*

The early Sages and the later Sages

Whether the Oral Law had been written down by the end of the *Mishnaic* period or not, in any event with the conclusion of the *Mishnah* a great epoch in the development of the law came to a close. Just as the Sages of the *Mishnah* had accepted that they have no power to abrogate Sinaitic law, [11] so the teachers of the Talmud considered themselves bound by the ruling of the *Mishnah*. [12] It appears that the later Sages felt that they did not possess the greatness of the earlier Sages and that therefore their power to act as law-makers was more limited. [13]

Throughout this book we have spoken of the contribution of the Sages to the Oral Law without reference to the character of the Sages who were the law makers. It would be well if in conclusion we made the remark that the greatness of the Sages to which we

11   See *ante* p. 109.
12   See *Kesef Mishneh, Mamrim* II, 1 : "Why do the *Amoraim* not dispute with the *Tannaim* ... ? It seems that after the conclusion of the *Mishnah* the later generations undertook not to dispute with the earlier generations. A similar thing occurred at the conclusion of the Talmud." After the conclusion of the Talmud, it was not even possible to enact new *Takkanot* and *Gezerot* for the whole of Jewry. See Maimonides, *Introduction to Mishneh Torah*.
13   The thought that earlier generations were greater is variously expressed in Talmudic literature. See "If the earlier generations were like angels we are like mere men" *Shabbat* 112B. "The heart of earlier generations was like the gate of the *Ulam* (20 *Amot*) and that of the later generations like the gate of the Temple (10 *Amot*)" *Erubin* 53A. See also *Yoma* 9B. See generally, Introduction to *Taamey Hamizvot* of Menaḥem of Rekanati by S. Lieberman (London, 1962) p. 20 *et. seq.*

have just referred did not lie in any particular office or appointment which they occupied or held, nor did it rest entirely on intellectual superiority or erudition. [14] More than that was required of the Sages "If the teacher is like an angel of God" said the Sages "seek Torah from him and if not do not seek Torah from him." [15]

A new theory why the Law was not to be put into writing

The emphasis laid upon the spiritual quality of the teachers of the Oral Law and not merely on the quality of their teaching is one of the more distinctive features of traditional Judaism. [16] It may also be one of the reasons why it was prohibited to write down the Oral Law. [17] The writing down of the law enables any scholar,

14 See *Sukkah* 28A (Soncino Talmud) "Hillel the elder had eighty disciples ... the greatest of them was Jonathan b. Uziel, the least of them Joḥanan b. Zakai. They said of R. Joḥanan b. Zakai that he did not leave unstudied Scripture, *Mishnah, Gemara, Halachah, Aggadah*, details of the Scribes ...

   They said of Jonathan b. Uziel that when he used to sit and occupy himself with the Torah, every bird that flew above him was immediately burnt. (It was like at Sinai when the Torah was given in fire — *Tosefot*.)

   Nothwithstanding R. Joḥanan's scholarship, the "greatest" was the pupil who possessed the "fire of Sinai."

15 *Ḥagigah* 15B.

16 This is also one of the important "parting of the ways" of the traditional attitude to the Oral Law from the attitude of such writers as I.H. Weiss, who heaps abuse upon great *Tannaim* throughout his work *Dor Dor V'dorshov* (e g. Vol. II, Chaps. 8 & 9, where he heaps abuse on R. Gamliel, R. Eliezar and R. Joshua).

17 See also *Sefer Ha'Ikarim* III, 23 and *Yam Shel Shlomo*, Introduction to *Ḥulin*, for suggestions why it was prohibited to commit Oral Law to writing.

whatever his character or his bias to present himself as an inter-
preter and teacher of the Oral Law. [18] On the other hand, when the
law is handed down orally, it is unlikely that teaching would be
accepted from anyone whose character is not such as to make his
tradition reliable. When there is no text against which it is possible
to check the law which is being taught, the complete integrity of
the teacher is the only assurance that what is being taught is not
pure invention and fabrication. It may be therefore that the prohibition against committing the Oral Law to writing was intended to
preserve the high spiritual qualities of the teachers of Oral Law.
This idea is possibly contained in the *Midrash*[19] which states: "God
said to Moses 'I will make you write most of my Torah but not all'
... because the *Mishnah* is the mystery of God, and God hands over
his mysteries only to the righteous."

18 Making Torah too widely and easily accessible is fraught with danger
and "Erez Israel shook for four hundred *parsa* by four hundred
parsa and a *Bat-Kol* came forth and demanded, 'Who has revealed
My secrets to men,' " when Jonathan b. Uziel first translated the
Prophets (*Megillah* 3A).
19 *Tanḥuma,* Vayera 6 (edit. Buber).

HEBREW SOURCES

SECTION I
THE FIRST MISHNAH ARRANGEMENT

3. Letter of Sherira Gaon I, 6

וספרא וספרי דרשי דקראי אינון והיכא רמיזא הלכתא בקראי, ומעיקרא
במקדש שני ביומי דרבנן קמאי לפום הדין אורחא הווי תני להון.

5. *Tosefta Eduyot* I, 1

כשנכנסו חכמים לכרם ביבנה אמרו עתידה שעה שיהא אדם מבקש דבר
מדברי תורה ואינו מוצא, מדברי סופרים ואינו מוצא, שנאמר (עמוס ח׳) הנה
ימים באים נאם ה׳ וגו׳ ישוטטו לבקש את דבר ה׳ ולא ימצאו ..... שלא יהא
דבר מדברי תורה דומה לחבירו. אמרו נתחיל מהלל ושמאי .....

8. *Sanhedrin* 86A

סתם מתני׳ ר׳ מאיר, סתם תוספתא ר׳ נחמיה, סתם ספרא ר׳ יהודה, סתם
ספרי ר״ש וכולהו אליבא דר״ע.

13. *Shaarey Teshubah* I, 20

מימות משה רבינו עד הלל הזקן היו שש מאות סדרי משנה כמו שנתנם
הקב״ה למשה בסיני, ומן הלל ואילך נתמעט ונתמסכן העולם וחלש כבודה
של תורה ולא תקנו מהלל ושמאי אלא ששה סדרים בלבד.

17.   I. I. Halevy, *Dorot Harishonim* I, 3 p. 206

והנה בית שמאי ובית הלל הם הנם הדור הראשון לתקופת התנאים, והם
הנם הראשונים אשר באו מהם במשנה מחלקאות ואשר מזה טעו לחשוב שהם
היו מיסדי ההלכה.

כי על כן עלינו רק לפתוח את ספר המשנה, לראות על מה ילכו שם כל
דבריהם.

לדוגמא במס׳ אהלות ז׳ משנה ג׳

"המת בבית ולו פתחים הרבה כולן טמאים נפתח אחד מהם הוא טמא וכולן
טהורים, חשב להוציאו באחד מהם או בחלון שהוא ארבעה על ארבעה
טפחים הציל על כל הפתחים.

בית שמאי אומרים והוא שחשב עד שלא ימות המת ובית הלל אומרים
אף משמת".

ומי לא יראה כי דברי בית שמאי ובית הלל אינם כי אם מה שנחלקו בפרוש
כונת דברי המשנה במה שנאמר בה "חשב להוציאו" *ש*בית שמאי סוברין
שהכונה שחשב עוד טרם שימות המת, ובית הלל מפרשים דין המשנה שהוא גם
בכל האופנים, וגם אם חשב משמת.

ומחלקאות כאלה יבואו לפנינו גם בדברי מפרשי המשנה, רק שדברי התנאים
בכל כיוצא בזה נקבעו אחר זה על המשנה ובאו לפנינו סדורים עמה יחד.

21.   Letter of Sherira Gaon I, 2

ולא הוו חד מן הראשונים דכתב מדעם עד סוף יומי דרבינו הקדוש. וכן
נמי לא הוו גרסי כולא בפה אחד ולשון אחד אלא טעמייהו הוו ידעין להון
וכולהון דעת אחת הוה בהון ולא הות בגרסייהו פלוגתא וידעי מאי דאיתיה
דברי הכל ומאי דאית ביה פלוגתא ומאי דאיתיה ליחיד ומאי דאיתיה לרבים
ולא היו להם דברים מתוקנים ומשנה ידוע שהכל שונני אותה בפה אחד ולשון
אחד. אלא אותן הטעמים והשמועות שהיו יודעין אע"פ שהחכמים כולן היו
שוין בהם, כל אחד ואחד מתני לתלמידיו באי זה חבור שירצה ובאיזה דרך
שירצה, יש שאוחז דרך קצרה ... ושקטו רבנן ביומי דרבי מכל שמדא משום
רחמנותא דאיכא בין אנטונינוס ורבי ואסכים לתרוצי הלכתא כי היכי דלגרסי
רבנן כולהו פה אחד ולשון אחד ולא לגרוס כל חד וחד לישנא לנפשיה.

SECTION II

CLARIFICATION OF THE ORAL LAW AT YABNEH

7. *Baba Mezia* 59B
   see *ante* p. 115.

8. *Berakhot* 27B

ת״ר מעשה בתלמיד אחד שבא לפני ר' יהושע, א״ל ״תפילת ערבית רשות
או חובה״ ? א׳-ל- ״רשות״. בא לפני רבן גמליאל א״ל ״תפילת ערבית רשות
או חובה ?״ א״ל ״חובה״. א״ל ״והלא ר״י אמר לי רשות״ א״ל ״המתן עד
שיכנסו בעלי תריסין לבית המדרש״ כשנכנסו בעלי תריסין עמד השואל
ושאל ״תפילת ערבית רשות או חובה״ ? א״ל ר״ג ״חובה״. אמר להם ר״ג
לחכמים ״כלום יש אדם שחולק בדבר זה״. אמר ליה ר״י ״לאו !״ א״ל ״והלא
משמך אמרו לי רשות !״ אמר ליה ״יהושע עמוד על רגליך ויעידו בך״.....
היה ר״ג יושב ודורש ור״י עומד על רגליו עד שרננו כל העם ואמרו לחוצפית
התורגמן ״עמוד !״ ועמד. אמרו ״עד כמה נצעריה וניזיל, בר״ה אשתקד צעריה,
בבכורות במעשה דר' צדוק צעריה, הכא נמי צעריה, תא ונעבריה !״,

9. *Tosefta Eduyot* I, 1 see *ante* p. 165.

THE REDACTION OF R. JUDAH HANASI

10. *Giṭṭin* 29A

מ ת נ י' המביא גט בא״י וחלה, ה״ז משלחו ביד אחר. ואם א״ל טול לי
הימנה חפץ פלוני, לא ישלחנו ביד אחר, שאין רצונו שיהא פקדונו ביד אחר.
ג מ ' אמר ר״ל כאן שנה רבי אין השואל רשאי להשאיל, ואין השוכר רשאי
להשכיר.

17. *Baba Ḳama* 102A

מ ת נ י': הנותן צמר..... לצבוע לו אדום וצבעו שחור, שחור וצבעו
אדום, ר״מ אומר נותן לו דמי צמרו, ר״י אומר אם השבח יתר על היציאה
נותן לו את היציאה, ואם היציאה יתירה על השבח נותן לו את השבח.

גמ': יתיבי רב הונא וקאמר..... והלכה כר"י..... אהדרינהו רב יוסף
לאפיה..... למה לי..... מחלוקת ואחר כך סתם הלכה כסתם! מחלוקת
בבבא קמא..... וסתם בבבא מציעא, דתנן כל המשנה ידו על התחתונה.....
ורב הונא? אצטריך, סד"א אין סדר למשנה וסתם ואחר כך מחלוקת היא.
ורב יוסף? אי הכי כל מחלוקת ואח"כ סתמא נימא אין סדר למשנה וסתם
ואח"כ מחלוקת היא. ורב הונא כי לא אמרינן אין סדר למשנה בחדא מסכתא
אבל בתרי מתסכתות אמרינן.

21. *Tosefot Yom Tov, Sotah* IX, 1

ותירצו (בתוספות) דאע"ג דלכולהו אמוראי בתרי מסכתות אין סדר ואין
הלכה כסתם ר' יוחנן אית ליה דאפילו בתרי מסכתות הלכה כסתם. דמסתמא
סתם לבסוף ואין לנו לומר שסתם רבי קודם ושוב חזר ממה שפסק ע"כ.....
נ"ל..... שהרמב"ם מתרץ קושית התוס' בכך דלהכי מקשה גמרא מסתם
דבנזיר אע"ג דמחלוקת היא בביצה משום דכיון דבתרי סדרי נינהו. ונזיר
בסדר נשים שאחר סדר מועד אמרינן דיש סדר והוה מחלוקת ואחר כך סתם
דהלכה כסתם. וטעמא רבה איכא דכיון דנקטינן בסידרייהו באסמכתא דקרא
(ישעיה ל"ג) "והיה אמונת עתך" "כדאיתא בפ"ב דשבת (דף לב) אית לן למימר
דכסדר האסמכתא למדם רבינו הקדוש..... ומיהו לדעת הרי"ף והרא"ש נמי
אין סדר אפילו בתרי סדרי.

INDEX OF SOURCES AND AUTHORITIES

(Including Bible, Mishnah, Talmudim, Rabbinic and other Jewish
and non-Jewish Sources.)